DRAMATIC PLAY
IN THE EARLY YEARS

Elizabeth Coffman

Pembroke Publishers Limited

*To Beth Albers-Jones, a teacher who truly understands the value
of dramatic play in the early years and the powerful insights
of children when they are invited into the story*

© **2015 Pembroke Publishers**
538 Hood Road
Markham, Ontario, Canada L3R 3K9
www.pembrokepublishers.com

Distributed in the U.S. by Stenhouse Publishers
480 Congress Street
Portland, ME 04101
www.stenhouse.com

Funded by the Government of Canada
Financé par le gouvernement du Canada | **Canada**

Library and Archives Canada Cataloguing in Publication

Coffman, Elizabeth, author
    Dramatic play in the early years / Elizabeth Coffman.

Includes bibliographical references and index.
Issued in print and electronic formats.
ISBN 978-1-55138-307-1 (paperback).--ISBN 978-1-55138-910-3 (pdf)

    1. Play. 2. Early childhood education--Activity programs.
3. Drama in education. I. Title.

| LB1139.35.P55C64 2015 | 372.21 | C2015-903651-8 |
| | | C2015-903652-6 |

Editor: Kate Revington
Cover Design: John Zehethofer
Typesetting: Jane Thornton

Printed and bound in Canada
9 8 7 6 5 4 3 2 1

FSC
www.fsc.org
MIX
Paper from
responsible sources
FSC® C004071

Contents

Introduction: Learning through Play Experiences *5*
Once upon a Time *5*
The Value of Play *6*
A Partnership between Teacher and Learners *7*
A Focus on the Thinking Required for Co-construction *9*
A Reflection of the Reggio Emilia Approach *9*
Acknowledgments *9*

Chapter 1: The Creative Process *10*
Before the *Aha* Moment *10*
Thinking Imaginatively *11*
Pausing to Reflect and Experiment *12*
Dramatic Play as Bodily Knowing *13*
The Creative Process at Work: Becoming Animals *13*
Your Role in the Creative Process *14*
How Dramatic Play Unfolds: Regaining the Castle *15*

Chapter 2: Beginning Dramatic Play *18*
Working as a Whole Group *18*
The Willing Suspension of Disbelief *19*
Assessing Children's Commitment *20*
A Good Start for a Story *21*
Warming Up to Play Together: Strategies *22*
Where Comprehension, Meaning, and Insight Meet: The Pause *23*
Listening for Next Steps *24*
The Benefits of Pausing Dramatic Play *25*
Your Role in the Beginning of Play *26*
How Dramatic Play Unfolds: Children as Rainforest Creatures *27*

Chapter 3: The Importance of Practice *29*
Working towards Focus and Control *30*
Physical Games and Activities to Promote Focus *31*
Drawing as an Exercise in Sustained Observation *33*
Side-Coaching *34*
Slow Motion Practice *36*
Your Role during Practice *36*
How Dramatic Play Unfolds: Practicing Their Way into Character *37*

Chapter 4: Building Belief *41*

Balancing Play Energy and Theatre Practice *41*
Using Space to Help Suspend Disbelief *42*
Using Narration to Cast a Spell *44*
Using Rumors to Promote Imagining *44*
Using Research to Provide Detail *45*
Augmenting Understanding through Art *46*
Building Belief through Use of Blank Paper *47*
Writing in Role and First-Person Singular *48*
Your Role in Building Belief *49*
How Dramatic Play Unfolds: Building Belief within a Story *50*

Chapter 5: Finding the Story *53*

Walking with Words: Working with a Story Text *53*
Staying inside the Story *55*
Choosing a Story *55*
Going Deeper: Experiencing Cinderella's Plight *56*
Ways to Expand Understanding *57*
Your Role within a Story *59*
Improvising a Story *60*
Prompting Improvisation: Strategies *61*
How Dramatic Play Unfolds: Expanding the Story of Icarus *62*

Chapter 6: Playing inside Curriculum *64*

Establishing a Framework for Investigation *64*
Getting into the Curriculum Story: Approaches *66*
Finding the Story in Social Studies *68*
Framing Historical Stories *70*
A Framework Example: Leaving Home for a New Life *71*
Experiencing History: Aboard *La Grande Hermine* *73*
Finding the Story in Science *74*
Exploring Living Things in Science: Becoming Butterflies *75*
How Dramatic Play Unfolds: Addressing Drought *77*

Chapter 7: Teacher in Role *79*

What Is a Formal Role? *80*
Planning for a Formal Role *80*
Your Role as Teacher in a Formal Role *83*
A Formal Role, Three Ways: Bully, Bystander, Bullied *84*
What Is an Interactive Role? *85*
Planning an Interactive Role *86*
How Dramatic Play Unfolds: The Timid Triceratops *87*

References *91*
Index *93*

Introduction: Learning through Play Experiences

The Grade 1 students were learning about fairy tales. Having immersed the children in all of the classics, the classroom teacher wondered what the children had actually absorbed. Did they have a grasp of the common elements found in fairy tales? Were they aware of the human characters and animals that helped and hindered? She was also curious about the children's ability to play together to create their own fairy tale. What themes and characters might they create? How could dramatic play provide an assessment of what they had learned? The teacher was well aware of the risk of entering into a whole-class dramatic play experience without preplanning the story and acting it out as they usually did, but she wanted to take the experience further. She invited a dramatist with lots of play experience to partner with her so that she could observe and document the children's experiences.

Once upon a Time

The Fairy Tale The dramatist showed the children four potentially magic symbols that she and the teacher had chosen ahead of time. The objects were a wand, a stone heart, a carved duck, and a feather. The children simply nodded in agreement that all of these items could be part of their story. The dramatist marvelled at their willingness to accept these as possibilities, while not knowing the story outcome. But how best to begin, she wondered . . . ?

Not having a beginning in mind is always an uncomfortable prospect for an adult, but trusting that children are capable of suggesting a beginning is an important element in dramatic play. Since the dramatist knew this, she simply asked how the students thought the story should begin. Suggestions followed until a child commented that they could play like they do at recess. Realizing that this was a perfect beginning that would include the whole class, the dramatist then took the next step. She asked the children for the first words of the story. With great enthusiasm, the whole class responded with "Once upon a time." So, with her best storytelling voice, she began:

"Once upon a time, a long, long time ago, there was a village full of children who loved to play."

She stopped and asked the children to show her how they were playing and what they might play. There was no need to discuss. They knew instantly what this beginning scene in their story would look like. The dramatist then began again, and this time the children responded, playing in small groups and pairs as if they were a well-rehearsed cast.

The children were, of course, noisy, which cued the dramatist for the next sentence. *"But the children were very noisy, and they knew that there was someone in their village who* hated *noisy children."*

The dramatist stopped again, wondering what the children might suggest next. Would their play get out of control? Would they argue and want to take hero or villain roles? Could they make decisions together as a group along the way? When she asked them who might not like all the noise, however, she realized that the fairy-tale themes they had been studying had been thoroughly absorbed.

"The witch!" they cried in unison, pointing to their classroom teacher. Of course, it was the witch! Could it be anyone else?

The dramatist realized how capable these children were in telling this unknown story together. She asked the children which symbolic object the witch would find most useful. One child picked up the wand and handed it to the classroom teacher without a word. When asked what the teacher-witch would do with the wand, one boy cried out, "She will turn us into robots and lock us in the dungeon!"

And thus the story began . . .

The Value of Play

Beyond the Wand

Within their fairy tale, the children used all four symbolic objects. Later, when held in a dungeon, they chose the wooden duck to help them escape. "He can peck the bars loose." When that failed, one child suggested that the duck (held by the dramatist) fly over to the snoring witch and steal a dangling key. Freed, the children raced away, but were asked to consider crossing a great river. This time they chose the feather, and one boy, feather in hand, flew each child across the water.

That left the stone heart. The dramatist asked the children what they might do with it. Without hesitation, one of them said, "The witch has lost her heart." They encircled the witch and as they passed the stone heart, each of them told her how her life would be better if she put back her heart. Moved by their appeals, the witch put back her heart, and the children cheered.

The fact that you have picked up this book on dramatic play suggests that you already sense the value of play in your classroom and are curious about how drama can enhance children's learning experiences. Let us first note some research findings.

Much has been written about the value of play. Government documents, such as *Early Returns: Manitoba's Early Learning and Child Care Curriculum Framework for Preschool Centres and Nursery Schools*, state clearly: "Play has intrinsic value far beyond a way to fill time. Play provides unlimited possibilities for learning and development" (Manitoba Child Care Program 2009, 6).

In the past, theorists such as Lev Vygotsky and John Dewey began a new dialogue about childhood, learning, and the vital role of play in supporting a healthy child.

Vygotsky (1978, 74) argued that "[i]n play the child is always behaving beyond his age, above his usual everyday behavior; in play he is, as it were, a head above himself. Play contains in a concentrated form, as in the focus of a magnifying glass, all developmental tendencies; it is as if the child tries to jump above his usual level."

Experience is an important component of how we shape dramatic play. As Dewey (1938, 43–44) points out in *Experience and Education*: "In an experience, interaction occurs between an individual, objects, and other people. The experience becomes what it is because of this transaction between an individual and what constitutes his or her environment. The environment consists of whatever conditions (objects or people) interact with an individual's internal personal needs, desires, capacities, and purposes that create the resulting experience."

Many researchers in the twenty-first century have further developed the views of Vygotsky and Dewey. For example, a report by McCain, Mustard, and Shanker (2007, 49) states: "Play: expands intelligence, is a testing ground for language and reasoning, connecting to the challenges children face in school, such as literacy, math, and science concepts, stimulates the imagination, encouraging creative problem solving, helps develop confidence, self-esteem, a sense of strengths and weaknesses, and a positive attitude toward learning, is a significant factor in brain and muscle development." It is not difficult to uncover a wide range of insights, theories, and good reasons for keeping play alive in the early years classroom.

Dramatic play as a natural response

Dramatic play is a unique and powerful way for children and teachers to partner in an active investigation of stories, big ideas, and events. Some of the simple forms of dramatic play will be familiar to you. Children become playful, for example, in response to a story as you are reading it. They may bark at the mention of a dog or groan if a character in the story groans. You may also observe parts of the story being re-enacted when children are playing independently. Whether it is a whole-group response to a story, a re-enactment in the play area, or a play created by a small group of students on their own, it is inevitable that dramatic play will emerge in the early years classroom as a natural response to learning.

A Partnership between Teacher and Learners

As in any good story, dramatic play includes a structure, participants, a physical environment, and things that happen, but, unlike independent play, it is a distinct form: a partnership between teacher and learners. Dramatic play is not to be confused with theatre. There is no set script, lines to be memorized, or audience to watch and listen. Dramatic play does, however, borrow from children's natural understanding of play and from the willing suspension of disbelief that we experience in all forms of effective theatre. Because dramatic play is about process rather than product or performance, the teacher is much involved in planning and playing with children in order to help them discover the complexities of the human journey and develop empathy towards others and themselves.

Most drama curricula state something like this: As students live through experiences of others in imagined situations, they learn to understand a variety of points of view and motives and to empathize with others. This exploration of the "as if" in roles and worlds will help students deepen their understanding of humanity and of issues of equity and social justice. Students will also learn to use language effectively to communicate a character's emotional state and point of view.

It is in the transaction that dramatic play heightens the learning experience. We cannot expect children to fully comprehend unless they experience their learning in ways that deepen their understanding. This is why dramatic play is such a valuable approach for children. It is about living through an experience. It invites children to explore their learning from *inside* the story, whether the story is familiar, historical, leading into a science investigation, or based on children's own experience. The difference between storytelling and dramatic play is in the children *becoming* the story, living the lives of the characters or animals, bumping up against the issues and tensions that the story brings into the foreground.

In *Story Drama*, David Booth (2005, 13) notes: "Drama may be one of the few language situations in school that opens up story possibilities, that allows spontaneous narrative to enter naturally into the flow of talk — every kind of story from personal experience to literary fictions — so that the narrative mode can be an integral part of the school curriculum."

Staying alert to story possibilities

Dramatic play, like any good piece of theatre, is a story told. Because the story emerges from a variety of places, the teacher, in planning for dramatic play, stays alert to story possibilities offered by the children that can lead into complex ideas worth living through. The story is investigated collaboratively, with the teacher co-constructing the unfolding of the story as she listens to the children, initiating the central tensions to be explored, stopping and starting as the story develops to consider the next steps.

Like written stories or scripts, dramatic play will have characters (animal, human, or otherwise) and something exciting that happens. Characters have attitudes and conversations, and there may even be some narration of the events as they unfold. Scenes that bring shifts and changes will be created. Costumes and props may be required as well, although they are often ordinary blocks and classroom objects used to represent a variety of things.

Dramatic play can be further developed by the teacher by borrowing from the art of theatre: children can be helped to willingly suspend their disbelief as they explore inside the story. By being aware of and using some of the skills involved in drama, such as expressive use of voice, characterization, movement, stillness, concentration, and listening, children can become more expressive in their play. Most children understand the importance of voice and movement in interpreting characters. Monsters with heavy feet, arms reaching out, and a big voice come readily to mind, but staying in the story in a focused way and constructing its direction with others is often what proves to be difficult.

Dealing with unknown outcomes

Dramatic play in the learning environment can be particularly challenging for adults who often feel obligated to focus entirely on outcomes. In dramatic play the outcome is often not known ahead of time. The main features of the story may form parts of the dramatic story, but the details, content, and responses are the children's. This characteristic represents a shift from the teacher-directed classroom to a place in which children's ideas, theories, and voices are respected and central to the experience. The teacher is the one who is curious, who observes, who facilitates, and who partners with the children in their play experience.

Letting go of full control and focus on outcomes can be difficult, but the rewards far outweigh the struggle to do so. Once children have had an opportunity to play together and have learned some of the basic skills involved in dramatic play, the dynamic of the classroom shifts, new voices are heard, learning is motivated by enthusiasm, and deeper understanding emerges.

> With a supportive environment and strategies in place, an educational culture of creativity can accommodate creative explorations where outcomes are largely unknown. This implies that parameters for learning experiences, designed for this environment, allow enough latitude for experimentation, idea generation, and potentially diverse outcomes. (Kelly and Leggo 2008, 31)

A Focus on the Thinking Required for Co-construction

Throughout this book, the focus is on the thinking essential for you to be a co-constructor with the children in dramatic play. You will be led from beginning steps to more challenging approaches, such as teacher in role. As you will see, however, the application approach in each chapter is really much more circular, with all of the ingredients in each chapter stirred together in every dramatic play event. In other words, the creative process is constantly at work, with efforts taken to practice each step of the way and to work towards the building of belief over and over again.

All seven chapters are organized in a step-by-step manner. Each chapter contains strategies; examples; an outline of your role; descriptions of dramatic play experiences, based on my own work with students; and a summary of key points. The accounts of dramatic play, which interweave through the chapters, will provide you with an authentic sense of the practice as experienced in an ordinary classroom with real children. In the book, I am also weaving in an image of the children I have encountered as competent, powerful storytellers.

Author as Dramatist

In the story experiences presented, I refer to myself as "the dramatist," as someone who brings a specific understanding of the blending of the elements of drama and of play to dramatic play experiences. The convention is meant to distinguish me from the teachers who welcomed me into their classrooms.

A Reflection of the Reggio Emilia Approach

The image of children as "rich," "strong," and "powerful" is key to the Reggio Emilia approach to early childhood education that first developed in Italy more than 40 years ago. That understanding is also central to this book.

Carla Rinaldi, president of Reggio Children, was interviewed by Lella Gandini. She said: "The cornerstone of our experience, based on practice, theory, and research, is the image of the child as rich in resources, strong, and competent. The emphasis is placed on seeing the children as unique individuals with rights rather than simply needs. They have potential, plasticity, openness, the desire to grow, curiosity, a sense of wonder and the desire to relate to other people and to communicate" (Edwards, Gandini, and Forman 1998, 114).

My experience with children in dramatic play has taught me that children are capable, interested, curious, and wanting to make meaningful connections with the world around them. The dramatic play experiences I outline will, I hope, inspire you to create more lived-through experiences in your own classroom, knowing that children love to play and that when they play, their wisdom guides us to understand more clearly who they are as learners.

Acknowledgments

Thanks to all the early years teachers who have invited me into their classrooms and let me play. In your classrooms, I have had the privilege of gaining a greater understanding of the beauty of children's imaginations which, I hope, I have reflected in this book. I especially thank Beth Albers-Jones, who has provided many opportunities for me to play with her and her students over the years.

1 The Creative Process

"Creativity is like wanting to know. Creativity is like digging deeper. Creativity is like looking twice. Creativity is like listening to smells. Creativity is like listening to a cat. Creativity is like crossing out mistakes. Creativity is like getting in deep water. Creativity is like having a ball. Creativity is like cutting holes to see through. Creativity is like cutting corners. Creativity is like plugging in the sun. Creativity is like building sand castles. Creativity is like singing in your own key. Creativity is like shaking hands with tomorrow."

— Paul Torrance, in an interview with Michael Shaughnessy

How many times have you said to the class "Be creative"? We say it because we want to inspire and urge children to be free. Sometimes, we say it because a child is stuck, and we hope that "be creative" will somehow fling open the door to something significant and remarkable. We often use "be creative" because we believe that children *are* creative and that all we have to do is remind them and the muse will suddenly manifest itself. Indeed, children are creative — no doubt about it — but being creative is a complex process much more involved than a half-hour activity or a visit to the craft table when their regular work is finished. In other words, creativity does not occur in a vacuum: it takes time and thought to achieve. Furthermore, the creative endeavor should be something that the children find meaningful.

Before the *Aha* Moment

We are, of course, familiar with the creative thinker who declares that "it suddenly came to me!" Such a moment is described as a flash of insight, as the *aha*, or eureka, moment. This perhaps is how we think of creativity: as a spur-of-the-moment awakening. Further exploration of this unique event, however, will reveal that much more is involved than a sudden flash of inspiration.

Research identifies a series of stages that the individual experiences before reaching the *aha* moment of revelation (some say four; others, five or six). Although the terminologies change from researcher to researcher, all agree that creativity involves a process of thinking long before the product comes to fruition. In 1926, Graham Wallas, a social psychologist, set out four major stages in the creative process that he noticed among artists and creative thinkers. These stages have become the reference point for much of the present-day research. The four stages are as follows:

- **Preparation** — The problem, question, or idea is investigated in all directions. Imaginative thinking is required.
- **Incubation** — Time is taken to think, ponder, reflect, and discuss.
- **Illumination** — Insight is gained; the *aha* moment is experienced. Regrouping may be necessary.
- **Verification** — The validity of the idea is tested. The project becomes visible.

In his book *The Art of Thought*, Wallas writes, "In the daily stream of thought these stages constantly overlap each other as we explore different problems" (1926, 38).

So, when we say, "be creative," we are really assuming that these four stages (or similar stages) have been put into place and that the children are ready for the final phase of verification, during which they may or may not produce something.

Dramatic play as a creative process

Dramatic play is very much a creative process for both you and the children. As in the first stage proposed by Wallas, it involves a problem that can be investigated in a great many directions. Dramatic play also gives children time to think, ponder, and reflect as the play process unfolds and the children want to talk about what just happened. For the teacher, the period of incubation provides the next steps in collaborating with the children to consider how the story might proceed. Illumination or *aha* moments will occur throughout as the children discover the difficulties and complications of the lived-through experience. They can gain illumination during the story, during the pauses, and at the end when the class may look back on the experience through writing and drawing to retell the story. Like illumination, verification occurs throughout dramatic play. Indeed, it is the reason why dramatic play can be an important factor in a child's learning: it consists of a constant testing of ideas as the children live through an experience together.

Thinking Imaginatively

Imagination and inspiration are major ingredients of the creative process. Imagination is the formation of a mental image while inspiration is what propels these thoughts into reality. The imagination, however, often requires and is prompted by ideas worth serious consideration. All of the research into the creative process underlines the importance of this initial stage of preparation. Ideas do not emerge from nowhere, and the imagination is more than just the problem-solving part of the brain — imagination is the brain's capacity to think in fresh, new ways, to turn things upside down and inside out, and to see from different perspectives. Ideas grow out of fertile ground that is enriched over time by consideration and exploration of a wide range of possibilities. It is the fertile ground of the imagination that plays such an important role in learning.

Encouraging imaginative thinking prompts children to play with ideas, solutions, and possibilities, to move outside conventional thinking to experiment with different approaches and take a different stance. The imagination stretches us into lifelong learning. It is what permeates dramatic play, encouraging children and teachers to explore the world and live through experiences of the "other."

Three Studies on Play

Bergen, Doris. 2001. "Pretend Play and Young Children's Development" (ERIC Digest No. EDO-PS-01). Champaign, IL: ERIC Clearinghouse on Elementary and Early Childhood Education.

Gray, Peter. 2011. "The Decline of Play and the Rise of Psychopathology in Children and Adolescents." *American Journal of Play* 3(Spring): 443–63.

Kalliala, Marjatta. 2006. *Play Culture in a Changing World.* Berkshire, UK: Open University Press.

If we can capture the imagination, then we have captured the child's capacity for learning.

As you enter into dramatic play it will be important to support and encourage multiple possibilities from the children. One of your main tasks throughout dramatic play is to provide children with material that stimulates the imagination and inspires their commitment and willingness to investigate further. In this period of idea generation, your own thinking will be challenged to move beyond predictability and outcomes; you will have to wrestle creatively with the big ideas that will carry dramatic play into worthwhile areas to explore with the children.

Pausing to Reflect and Experiment

Pausing is very much part of the creative process. It gives children time to reflect on what has just happened; it also gives them time to consider other options and ideas, to regroup if necessary, to try another angle, or to gather more information.

What often emerges from the discussion during the pause may seem risky as the next step in the dramatic story. Dramatic play, however, is an opportunity for children to take a risk in order to understand it more fully. Risk taking and trial and error are central ingredients in the creative process for both children and adults. Without the confidence to take a risk and try things out, we would probably never discover our own capabilities. Many recent investigations of play comment on the fear of risk at home and at school. Safety, both physical and psychological, is a concern, of course, but risk within a safe environment is perhaps the only way that learning can really take place. Risk, however, need not be about making mistakes. Taking a risk is the willingness to enter into the unknown — precisely where dramatic play can take you.

Risks taken in dramatic play are often the teacher's risks rather than the children's. It may feel risky to address big issues not normally discussed in the classroom. These issues include death, prison, divorce, racism, and violence. Nonetheless, these topics may represent what the children are experiencing or what they are curious about. It may be necessary to carefully explore big issues through dramatic play in order for children to make sense of their experiences.

The outcome in dramatic play is seldom known ahead of time. Not knowing the outcome can be unnerving for some teachers since it involves relying on one's own creative thinking along with that of the children and attending to the flow of events, constantly wondering where to next, like the artist exploring new material, unsure of where it will lead. Most early years teachers, however, come to know the exhilarating sense of playfulness that develops once self-consciousness is set aside.

The creative process takes time. When we invite children to "be creative," it is often with the notion that time is of the essence and the project must be completed within a given period. One important aspect of any creative endeavor is slowing down the process. Because dramatic play is less linear than, say, reading a story or exploring a math concept, and more of a spiraling of events, there is an automatic slowing down as children enter into an experience, and that experience informs the next steps. Pausing to reflect becomes part of the rhythm of creative work in play, and it is in the pause that the experience is enriched.

Dramatic Play as Bodily Knowing

Dramatic play is a physically creative activity. For children this involves somatic knowing, or what some might call the "embodiment of experience." When we say, "I know it in my bones," we are really referring to a bodily knowing that gives us a sense of complete knowing. This kind of knowing is different from that of the kinesthetic learner since it involves not just the need to move in order to understand but the need to understand through the body and the senses.

Having children engage in this kind of active participation can feel risky for teachers who are used to uniformity and control with children. Inviting children to move and express themselves through their bodies in a dramatic experience is not the same as in dance or gym. In dramatic play the children are thinking through the physical. In order to do this, they must take a whole-body approach rather than simply engaging in an intellectual thinking process. This is where dramatic play borrows from the actor's tool box: we can discover our expressive nature as we learn to feel in our bodies. The actor stays in control, studies actions, and puts her whole bodily self into the story. These factors are important to dramatic play.

Generating ideas, taking risks, and pausing for reflection are more important in creative work than the development of skills, such as staying in control or the expressive use of voice, especially as children explore what they know and how they know through their bodies. Although the dramatic play experience borrows from the skills required in theatre, its central focus is play. Skills, therefore, should simply be seen as the means to focus and communicate more effectively.

The following section provides an illustration of how the four key stages of the creative process look within a realistic dramatic play experience.

The Creative Process at Work: Becoming Animals

Your Grade 2 class is very interested in animals. They are fond of drawing them and listening to stories about them. You believe that they would be interested in being the animals as you have observed a number of them at the sand table playing stories with the plastic animals. In the back of your mind, you also are thinking that you could encourage them to think about habitat and environment if they were to enter into a dramatic play experience.

You invite the class to become animals. Without exception they accept and do so with enthusiasm. (Sometimes, however, a child does not want to participate right away but will join in later, not wanting to be left out of the fun.)

Initial Preparation: You brainstorm with the children, curious about which animals they will choose and what they know about them. A period of research follows as the children gather information and discover more about their chosen animals. You note much enthusiasm and the building of momentum.

Illumination: When you think the students have collected enough information, you gather them on the carpet for a discussion about their animals. You listen as they share what they have learned and generate ideas for a possible beginning for a dramatic story. During the discussion, children talk about something several of them saw on television about cities taking over spaces where animals used to live. You realize that this might be the beginning of a dramatic story, but more research is required. You ask a librarian to find some story and factual books about habitat. More preparation is required.

Incubation: Reading the stories and fact books with the children has given the children's initial thoughts on habitat time to simmer.

You recognize that as the children prepare to become their animals, the next step will be very physical. Spiraling back to the preparation stage of the creative process, you ask them to find a space in which they can work without hindrance from others. As you coach them from head to toe to become their animal, you watch carefully, noticing which children are focused and concentrating. The process feels risky and takes time, but after several practices and some trial and error, you can see that the children are bodily in their animal skins.

You then invite the children as animals to take the next step: to move around the classroom. All the while, you are observing, side-coaching, pausing to discuss, regroup, and refine. You recognize that this preparation is verification that they are ready to begin.

You realize, however, that you need to be part of the story. You announce that you are a great horned owl. Even though the children laugh at your owl interpretation, you recognize that you, too, have a sense of fun and anticipation about how the story will unfold.

You ask the children where they might begin the story in the classroom. Many ideas are generated, but they finally all agree that the story will begin with them in their dens, homes, or nests.

Preparation and Verification: As the children scramble to find particular places as their homes, you notice that they are no longer focused as animals, so you call them back as a group. They then practice their animals until they are satisfied that they are believable. "Where is your house?" one of the children asks. You realize that they want you to be in the story, too, so you put all embarrassment aside and climb up on a chair, hooting as you do so. The children are delighted! You hope that the principal does not drop in . . .

Your Role in the Creative Process

You play a facilitating role, not a laissez-faire one, throughout the creative process. As Robert Kelly and Carl Leggo write in *Creative Expression, Creative Education*: ". . . when it comes to developing a creative disposition in young learners, a complete laissez-faire approach to education is not the answer either. This assumes that students have complete sets of mature creative attributes . . . But these attributes have to be developed and practiced if they are to evolve into more sophisticated creative practices . . ." (2008, 23).

Children need to understand the process, and they definitely need to learn how to discuss ideas, listen to one another, and work and play together. You are central in all of these areas but without being directive in terms of the content. Dramatic play demands a unique balance between knowing when to steer and knowing when to be completely open to the children. As a familiar parallel, consider how you contribute to the reading and writing processes: you step in to provide the necessary support in order for the child to progress and you step back in order to observe the child's own meaning making.

You will also need to think in fresh, flexible ways, be able to put aside your own ideas, and let go of specific outcomes. Your role requires that you be willing to take risks and try things out with the children. This requirement can be quite challenging to meet, especially if you have always done things a certain way. In the creative process, you become a co-constructor of the dramatic story, working step by step as the play unfolds.

Perhaps the most important stance to take is an open one. An open stance relies on listening to children and on being curious about their ideas, suggestions, and theories while being able to construct with them the next steps that will continue the story. Research and planning will remain the primary roles you play as you progress in partnership with the children.

You can see the whole interview at http://www.naeyc.org/content/conversation-vivian-gussin-paley.

As distinguished early education researcher Vivian Paley said in an interview: "Think dramatically. Get in the habit of thinking of yourself and the children as partners in an acting company. Once we learn to imagine ourselves as characters in a story, a particular set of events expands in all directions. We find ourselves being kinder and more respectful to one another because our options have grown in intimacy, humor, and literary flavor."

How Dramatic Play Unfolds: Regaining the Castle

It was June and the children in the Grade 4/5 class were in play mode. Recognizing this shift in their focus, their teacher invited the dramatist into the classroom to explore a very open-ended dramatic story. The children had many suggestions for the theme of the play — everything from zombies to explorers in outer space. Many of the ideas were good, but not until one child suggested that the story take place in medieval times did consensus begin to build. Beyond that, the dramatist began to imagine a wide range of possibilities that would take the children outside their usual TV and video game scenarios. The children were instantly curious about medieval times, wondering out loud when and where medieval life took place.

Regaining the Castle, Part 1

One student suggested that the story begin in 1242. Class members all agreed and shared briefly what they knew about this time period. Some information was more accurate than other information, but the dramatist and the teacher were confident that with further research, the children would gain a clearer picture of medieval times.

Developing the story through drawing

The dramatist then placed a large sheet of blank paper in the middle of the carpet and drew a wavy line across the page. *"I know there is a river nearby,"* she said, *"but I am not certain about our location."* Without hesitation one of the students pointed to the top corner of the page and stated firmly, "We are here, north of the river." Another child added, "We are in a burned-out house next to the cathedral." It was obvious that the children were engaged.

Within seconds, another child pointed to the castle, informing us that it had been taken over by another king, but we had escaped. As the paper filled in with details — the castle, a forest, rocks, and hills — the tension of the story began to rise.

Identifying characters

Pausing to agree on the details colored-in the story further. The Grey Man and his men had taken over the castle. The princess and her retinue were among those who had escaped. Gradually, there emerged other roles: knights, servants, ladies-in-waiting, even a vagabond. The dramatist played with the children as part of the group, worrying with them and asking questions to work through various plots, waiting for the one in which the whole class could participate.

Learning about castle life

In the days that followed, the classroom teacher encouraged the students to find out more about castles and the people who lived in them. The students drew pictures, mapped out a castle, established their location in it, and wrote backstories about themselves, filling in much of the detail of the time period. When the dramatist returned, they had a rich store of detailed information to draw upon. Ideas they had generated about who they were had incubated sufficiently, and their imaginations were primed with pictures and stories. The class was ready to be in role and to address the problem of regaining their castle.

From fiery distractions to secret tunnels — trying out solutions

During this play session the problem was explored in every direction. The dramatist played one of the group, wondering and questioning; she later switched roles to be one of the castle guards.

Possible solutions for taking back the castle ranged far and wide. Could the soldiers who guarded the castle be distracted? The children decided that they would gather wood and make a huge fire to distract the guards. Once the guards (the classroom teacher and the dramatist) left their posts to investigate, they would be able to enter the castle. After a flurry of activity miming the loading of wood onto a cart and the lighting of a fire, the children realized their failure. The guards were only curious about the large fire — they did not leave their posts — and the children returned to their burned-out house to regroup. At this point, the dramatist returned to her role as one of the group and the teacher, to her work as observer outside the story.

Since dramatic play affords experimenting and also makes a story difficult rather than simple, these Grade 4/5 students were willing to try another scheme. This time the princess stepped forward to suggest that she knew of a secret passage. (There is always a secret passage!) Its opening was located a distance away, but the underground passage ended up in her bedroom under her bed, where there was a key that opened another secret passage inside the castle. She pointed to it on the map, and we were convinced.

Of course, the next part of our story focused on the passage. And so it was that the children rearranged the tables and chairs in the classroom, and the teachers draped them with large sheets of cloth. The children found crawling through the tunnel exciting, taking several practices so that everyone had a turn and no one stalled in the tunnel. The teacher later used the tunnel as a place for the children to crawl inside and write the next chapter of their story.

The story continued over the next few days with a visit from the principal as the Grey Man. The principal had been primed ahead of time by the classroom teacher to be stubborn and not give in. A debate over who actually owned the castle ensued, the Grey Man insisting on his rights and the students on theirs. Frustrated, the students gave up, and the Grey Man returned to the castle (the principal's office).

Finally, the children devised a plot to distract the Grey Man's castle guards (now played by the school secretaries). While the guards focused their attention on well-placed jewels, the original castle residents, the teacher and dramatist now among them, slipped down the hallway and stormed the castle — the principal's office. The principal was gently captured and pushed out onto the playground amid cheers from the class, whose members then made a joyous return to their castle.

The fluid playing of roles

As "Regaining the Castle" illustrates, the teacher often switches roles in dramatic play. Doing so may seem unconventional to adults, but children are already familiar with role switching in their own play experiences.

Other adults, too, are sometimes required to play roles within the story, a phenomenon very much part of children's play experiences, in which playing is fluid. A teaching assistant may be required to take on a role in conversation with the teacher as the children listen in. School secretaries are often delighted to participate in pirates' quests for treasure, frightened by their fierce demands. It is the sign of a healthy school when administrators, along with support staff and teachers, can play imaginatively with children.

The fruit of creative energy

No one knew how this story would unfold until it was finished, and we could tell it back in detail. The children's rich imaginations and creative energy as a group carried it forward with a classic understanding of how story works and who they could be as major players in it. The children, teacher, and dramatist all took a risk, working together to let the story unfold, exploring as they went along. In the end, though, they discovered the power and capacity of the imagination to live inside an experience, to say nothing of the delight of sneaking down the hall and invading the principal's office!

SUMMARY

When you launch a creative activity, be sure to do the following:
- Spend time discussing the idea or problem, looking at it from a variety of perspectives.
- Choose a beginning point that allows room for all the children to participate.
- Encourage children to play with ideas, solutions, and possibilities.
- Move beyond conventional thinking and be willing to take risks.
- Listen and observe to plan the next steps.
- Pause for reflection and discussion, and to regroup throughout the play experience. Let the experience incubate.
- Allow for thinking physically.
- Stay open to possibilities and ideas that you and your students have never thought of before — the *aha* moment.

2 Beginning Dramatic Play

"Play nourishes every aspect of children's development. It forms the foundation of intellectual, social, physical and emotional skills necessary for success in school and in life."
— Jane Hewes, *Let the Children Play* (p. 2)

Dramatic play is about process rather than product. It is about planning play experiences not just for, but *with* children that will invite them to explore and try out many situations in order to grow their own ideas and perceptions and develop empathy for and understanding of others and, indeed, themselves. Much like independent play, dramatic play gives children an opportunity to explore and experience situations in a safe environment that is "not for real." The "not for real" aspect of play allows you and the children to examine all sides of the story: to look between the lines, take a different approach, try out someone else's experience, "walk in another person's shoes," and move back and forth in time.

Unlike your role in students' independent play, where you may be an observer and note taker, here your role will shift to that of an equal participant in role with the children. Doing this can feel strange at first, especially for those of us who have forgotten the pure joy of play. You may find yourself cawing like a crow or taking on the role of the stern queen who disregards her subjects.

At the same time, however, you will engage your teacher-self, listening carefully for possible next steps that will deepen the children's experience. You will also need to know when to pause for further reflection, discussion, or planning; when to regroup or re-launch, in case the children want to make significant changes to their story; and when to enable the children to do more research in order to fully understand the situation.

Working as a Whole Group

Dramatic play functions best when the whole class is involved. As the Board of Studies New South Wales expresses it in *Creative Arts K–6 Syllabus, Early Stage 1*: "Young children may find it difficult to work dramatically in small groups, unless this is carefully structured by the teacher; however, they are likely to have fewer problems when asked to work as a whole group. Don't expect too much by way of sophisticated enactment. This is a complex task for young children" (2006, 104).

It can be challenging to achieve effective whole-class involvement when children have varying degrees of imaginative play experience together as a whole group. You may find that your class requires much more warming-up practice in order to understand this kind of physical, interactive invitation to play together. A sense of community can, however, develop from the dramatic play experience, making it worth pursuing even with the most dysfunctional group of children.

Working closely with your students, taking small steps with them as the dramatic story first unfolds, and assessing their focus and commitment will be especially important in the beginning phase of dramatic play; slowing down and backing up in order for children to fully understand what the willing suspension of disbelief means in their group play is also essential. It takes time and, as in all learning situations, taking time to explore, practice, and assess in order to determine the next steps is important in a whole-class dramatic play experience.

In dramatic play the teacher selects a beginning that will provide the excitement and momentum for the students to discover more and that will support and deepen further exploration as they research to clarify and expand on their story. As recorded in "How Dramatic Play Unfolds" in Chapter 1, the children initially offered many ideas about the year 1242. Some ideas were accurate and some were not. As they researched the medieval period, however, they not only gained a clearer picture of who they were and how they might have lived in the castle, but also discovered more details and possibilities for the lived-through experience.

The responses to the story beginning and the subsequent events are the children's. This aspect of dramatic play is often the most difficult for teachers to deal with. Dramatic play is open-ended. It relies on your listening and your trust in the children's innate wisdom. You need to stay open to direction from the students and to use their responses to co-construct the next steps, trusting in their insights and imagination.

The Willing Suspension of Disbelief

The beginning of any dramatic play experience draws heavily on the one main component from theatre: the willing suspension of disbelief. This imaginative process allows us to live through an experience with the actors as they reveal the story. It is also vital to a successful dramatic play experience as the story is revealed through the children's play.

Willingly suspending disbelief is often easy for five-, six-, and seven-year olds because imaginative play is still very much part of their play experience. They can quickly slip in and out of a role, acquire a different voice, prance like a pony, and imagine a flight to Mars with little effort. Students in Grades 3 and 4 require a little more time, sometimes with shorter periods to play inside a story. With older children, however, discussion during the pause can be rich and insightful as they talk about their feelings and observe the dynamics of the group.

Young students can readily apply themselves to dramatic play, but as you will discover in the following chapters, there are ways to help ensure that they suspend their disbelief.

Becoming geese, growing in credibility

The Lost Goose, Part 1

A Kindergarten class had been studying the geese on the pond near their school. The dramatist who was partnering with the classroom teacher asked the students if they would like to be geese. Of course, they did! They immediately took up various positions of flight and flew around the classroom, albeit in chaotic fashion.

The classroom teacher worried that the children were perhaps not ready to play together dramatically, but the dramatist assured her that this was an opportunity for the children to practice playing as a group. Since this was the class's first time playing dramatically together, the dramatist expected the children to require a few more practices before they could stay focused and sustain their play.

Calling them back to the carpet, the dramatist invited the students to do their best to believe that they were a flock of geese on a pond. They agreed to do so in unison. They were then prompted to stand on the spot to practice being believable as geese.

This invitation provided an opportunity to assess who was willing to suspend their disbelief and be inside the beginning of this story and who needed more support. It took several attempts until they agreed that they could believe themselves to be geese. They then discussed how geese fly together.

Side-coaching is described in greater detail in Chapter 3.

Another practice in a "V" formation ensued with little success. The dramatist decided that formation was perhaps too challenging for five-year-olds and instead invited the children to simply fly down the hallway and back to their pond. All the time they did this, she side-coached and encouraged their attempts, observing and assessing their credibility. The students as geese flew together and landed on their pond with some success.

It was important for the Kindergarten students to be the geese even before the story began. Without the practice and the check-in to see whether they could believe in themselves, the credibility of whatever was to happen in the story would be limited. It is interesting to note that, in this beginning phase of practice, the children did not see repeating the action several times as boring or wasted. The effort was all very much part of the dramatic play experience, which is most often the case.

Assessing Children's Commitment

Once you have involved the children in a beginning, perhaps calling upon them to be something or someone, you need to assess the children's commitment and ability. Are they in the story already? Who is struggling to stay focused?

For a first-time experience the whole notion of getting up out of chairs and moving around the classroom may require much practice. As in any first-time learning experience, children may not know what is expected of them. Getting up and moving around as another character is an exciting prospect. Being in a role takes imagination and focus. It may also require support and enrichment. Children may need exposure to related pictures, videos, stories, and discussion even before they move in order to gain a clear image of who, where, or what they are pretending to be and to begin to imagine. Rather than giving up on the children if the initial experience is chaotic, regard their attempt as an opportunity to develop a cohesive sense of community: they can learn to work together in a common story, listening to one another, sharing ideas, and planning together.

Waiting for the children to become invested in the story may take much patience on your part at the beginning. You may first have to wade through silly responses as they test this new learning territory. Of course, if they do not readily commit, you do not have to continue, but you may choose to persevere as you would in any learning situation in which children struggle.

A Good Start for a Story

The Lost Goose, Part 2

The children had seen a dead goose by the pond and there was much speculating about why and how it might have died. The teacher and the dramatist sensed that this event might be a good place for a story to begin. As the children as geese met again on the pond, the dramatist presented the problem: someone was missing. The children readily accepted this and began to share their theories. Their responses were wide ranging and often silly. The dialogue degenerated into wild and strange possibilities. With each response the dramatist tried to keep the children in the story rather than stopping to address the silliness. A child suggested that the missing goose had been murdered, and the others laughed.

Knowing that an effective beginning depended on establishing the willing suspension of disbelief, the dramatist accepted the child's comment with seriousness. She used her saddest voice and expressed fear and trepidation that someone might be hunting out of season and that they were all vulnerable. Several other children stated that they thought the goose had flown to Mars or gone for a burger.

How the Goose Was Found

Later on, despite many clues, the children were getting nowhere finding the goose, so the dramatist and classroom teacher introduced something new: a puppet goose from another classroom. The dramatist put the goose high on a shelf and suggested that the teacher play the role of a mean turtle using a large toy from the classroom collection. When the children discovered the goose, they rushed to get it, but the teacher as turtle announced that the goose was its captive. It seemed that the turtle wanted to fly and had captured the goose in order to learn. Of course, one goose child, soon followed by others, said she would teach the turtle. As students as geese took turns flying around with the turtle, the rescued goose expressed her gratefulness to the flock.

Again, staying in role and in the story, the dramatist accepted the response in an effort to draw the children into a serious deliberation about their missing friend. She made comments like these: *"I know we have talked about flying to Mars, but I understand that there is no food or water there so I hope he didn't try." "How many times have we talked about eating human food? Oh dear! I do hope he remembers not to."*

In creating a dramatic story with children, it is important to stay in the story at the beginning and encourage the group to move more deeply into the lived experience so that it can be felt. At the beginning neither classroom teacher nor dramatist knew how the story would evolve, but they trusted that the children would gradually come around.

And they did. All it took was one child saying, "Maybe he is lost and we should go and look for him." This was the moment the dramatist had been waiting for. She flagged this comment, recognizing that it had potential for the next step in the story. For these five-year-olds, the idea of the missing goose and the challenge to find out what had happened to it came to be seen as a worthy investment in dramatic play.

Integrating child contributions, inviting deeper responses

Staying in the story at the beginning and not giving up too quickly is an acquired skill: it comes with practice for both you and the children. Children lose interest quickly if you constantly come out of the story to address child comments that do not seem suitable to you. For many children the open-ended nature of dramatic play is a new and rare experience, so it may take a little imaginative work for them to believe in the story that they are invited to live through. It is a delicate balance to honor the child's sense of humor while at the same time ensuring that the group is willing to genuinely believe in the story.

It takes practice on your part to accept the child's contribution and keep it in the story while also inviting a more thoughtful response. Sometimes, all it takes is a recognition of what the child has contributed by addressing your comment to the character the child plays in the story. *"Mr. Bear, you always have a good sense of humor." "Yes, I know that you knights are wanting to blow things up, but we just don't have anything we can use."* This effort is all part of learning to play together and live inside a story with a willing suspension of disbelief.

The beginning of the dramatic play experience needs to be big enough and important enough that the children, with practice, of course, will want to invest time and energy in the experience. There needs to be enough tension to hold their interest and enough mystery that it will feel like a lived-through experience in which no one knows exactly what the outcome will be. Asking yourself what lived-through experience will deepen the children's learning is the first step to planning. Once you adopt this frame of mind, you will find no end of possibilities for dramatic play.

Warming Up to Play Together: Strategies

Even before you take the next steps in dramatic play, you may want to use and repeat a warm-up activity, such as one of those below, several times. The intent is for you and the children to be satisfied that the physical experience is focused and controlled. Especially if dramatic play is new to your class and you are unsure of how well the children can keep focus or stay in control, using stillness is an excellent way to warm up your class and prepare them for dramatic play. Here are a few activities that require stillness.

Freeze Frame

Having students practice stillness in a "freeze frame" gives you an opportunity to assess how they are handling this very physical experience and can provide you with direction for next steps. Indeed, Freeze Frame might be the way in which you begin each dramatic play experience, signaling to the students that they are now engaged in a very different way of working.

Freeze Frame can be done in a variety of ways that require children to stop and freeze at the sound of a drum, a hand clap, or any other agreed-upon signal. Being able to freeze and stay still can be quite a challenge for some children, but it is worth attempting. You may invite the class to create a pose on the spot that expresses a certain action or feeling using their whole bodies. At the sound of the drum, the children freeze in position. Or they may demonstrate a particular action required in their story, perhaps climbing a tree, crossing a fast-moving river, or hiding. Freezing in position is an opportunity to physically convey that part of the story.

Sculptor and Clay

Asking children to work in partners — one as the sculptor and one as the clay — is one way of getting children to pay attention to the wide range of physically expressive possibilities in stillness. You may ask the children to make visible a character's particular feeling or attitude in a story by having one child sculpt the other child in a position he thinks reveals the story best. Like Freeze Frame,

Sculptor and Clay can also be a way for children to demonstrate a particular action, with one partner modeling it.

In the sculpting activity, there is usually much discussion between the two children as they determine what the position should be. This exercise also helps them understand how the whole body has to express the particular attitude or action in order for any spectator to believe it.

Mirrors

Mirrors is also a common drama warm-up activity that requires co-operation and concentration. Two children stand opposite, facing each other. One leads; the other follows. The leader, using only arms and hands, makes wide, slow motions so that the follower can follow. The idea is for the follower to concentrate on the slow movements of the leader so that no one can tell who is leading and who is following. Having another student move among the pairs to see if she can identify each leader and follower adds a challenging dimension.

Where Comprehension, Meaning, and Insight Meet: The Pause

Stopping to reflect or pausing the dramatic play experience could easily be the single most important reason for the dramatist to enter dramatic play. Pausing is as important in dramatic play as the play itself. It gives children time to take stock of what they have just experienced, but it also gives time for you to listen for the next possible steps.

It is in the pause that comprehension, meaning, and insight come together. The children look back on the moment they have lived through to grapple with the feelings it evoked and the event's significance as the people or animals might have experienced it. During this discussion, plans for the next steps can emerge as you consider the dramatic potential of the children's reflections. This process of reflection often takes time and requires a genuine interest on your part. In the geese story, for example, the dramatist waited for the surfacing of an idea with the potential for the next step in dramatic play: something that would carry the story forward into areas of consideration.

Because dramatic play is about process rather than product, the goal of the dramatist is to recognize places in a story that might require further reflection outside the drama. Pausing can allow you to engage the children in a deeper conversation about what is happening and to redirect ideas, if necessary. It is important when the children get off track, exploring far too many ideas in their attempts to solve the problem or resolve the situation. It is helpful when the story has been intense and requires debriefing. Of course, pausing is also necessary if the children need to discuss and plan the next steps in the story.

Agreeing on an action or a signal for pausing the drama before the drama even begins is good practice. This is especially so for Kindergarten and Grade 1 students who find it difficult to stop playing! By pausing the drama you can keep in touch with what is going on for the children. A pattern on a drum, calling "freeze," taking off your hat, changing your position, or saying, "Let's stop and gather on the carpet to talk about what's happened so far" may be sufficient.

Pausing is also a key way for you to deal with problems or ideas that may be difficult for the children or that may need to be discussed further on in the dramatic play experience. For example, a pause may be necessary if the children choose a violent action to solve their dilemma. Discussing the consequences, along with the reality of their situation, gives them an opportunity to deliberate over right and wrong, continuing the story or ending it quickly, and addressing real-life circumstances as opposed to cartoon solutions.

Deciding to pause near the beginning of a story is always delicate — you will have to determine whether stopping will impede or refocus the children's investment in the story. In the goose story the dramatist made a conscious decision to remain in the story at the beginning even when the comments were silly, in order to build momentum and wait for the next step to emerge from the children's discussion. You will have to decide if stopping is necessary at the beginning of the story or if, by legitimizing the children's responses, you will draw them further into a believable lived-through experience.

You may want to stop briefly if a child presents an idea that does not quite fit the story or a group of students want to develop an idea on their own. For example, several children might want to form a delegation to present a petition. This initiative is worth discussing with the whole group, which can offer ideas for petition content as well as giving the delegation advice on how to deliver the petition. Pausing to discuss this idea with the whole group is an important part of the dramatic process.

Cause for pause: A common illustration

In one instance, the students playing prisoners decided to tempt the evil person guarding their room (the dramatist) with a glass of water, hoping that while she drank it, they could sneak away the key she held close by.

A class has just begun their story. The children understand that they are being held captive by an evil person and must plot an escape. They have gathered in the darkest of the night to whisper possible ways that they might get out of their predicament. Nearly all of the suggestions they make involve magical powers, weapons, and explosives.

The teacher listens for a while and then stops the story. In the pause, she reminds them of their circumstances and asks them what would be more interesting: to use magic and escape immediately (the story would then be over) or to try a variety of solutions based on their actual situation. The children opt for the latter, recognizing that to play on is far more exciting. They continue playing out their night-time meeting, this time making more realistic suggestions.

Listening for Next Steps

Tuning in to the children's responses and waiting for the next step to emerge is the single most difficult aspect of playing with children. Doing this requires a very different kind of listening than you usually do as a teacher since you are not planning the outcome or the rest of the story; rather, you are listening for possible next steps to take.

Three ways to listen

There are three ways in which you can listen for next steps: (1) by waiting for an opportunity to emerge during the children's role-playing inside the story, (2) by asking "what's next?" and (3) by listening to and joining in the children's discussion during a pause to decide with them what the next part of the story might contain and how it might proceed.

1. **During role playing.** More often than not, the next steps in the story pop up while the children are playing their roles inside the story, particularly in a gathering or meeting as the children confront the initial problem, as they did in the goose story and as you will see in other classroom experiences outlined in this book. Listening for these opportunities may take some practice on your part as you consider whether or not the child's suggestion has merit in furthering the story. In the goose story, the child's suggestion that the goose was lost opened up a number of possibilities for a search, looking for clues, and deciding what was a clue and what wasn't; it also pointed to the bigger notion of group solidarity and concern for the welfare of one of their own. When you can see a range of active possibilities, it is probably a good indication of the next step to take.

2. **Taking the direct approach.** Pausing the initial play experience to ask "What's next?" provides stepping stones as you and the children proceed step by step through the story. Using this approach gives children time to gather ideas and together consider what the next best step might be. It also provides children with time to practice the suggestion and decide whether it should be part of the story. This approach is a kind of practice as you go: you establish a beginning point, the children play it out, you stop and ask what should happen next, they discuss it and choose to try a next event, and then you stop again and consider with them whether to make this part of the story or try another angle. This approach lends itself nicely to thoughtful consideration of the many avenues into story that are part of the creative process.

3. **Pausing for discussion.** Sometimes, the next step is the result of pausing or stopping the story when the children confront a particularly difficult issue that you think requires further consideration. A thread worth pursuing often surfaces from discussion. Pausing in this way can be a useful strategy to deepen the lived-through experience and to generate ideas that further the dramatic play story.

The Benefits of Pausing Dramatic Play

Each of the following three examples of classroom experiences points to a different advantage to pausing the dramatic play action: to promote discussion and planning, to deepen understanding, and to gather information.

Pausing for discussion and planning: How to scare off encroaching humans

The Grade 4 students were being animals in a forest and a lumber company was fast encroaching on their habitat. They had gathered to consider their options and had made many great suggestions.

"We could pretend to be a huge monster and scare the workers away," one child suggested.

"How would we do that, I wonder? Any suggestions?" asked the dramatist.

The Grade 4 students sincerely applied themselves to the child's possible solution and ended up creating a very large group sculpture, with some students standing on a table and others acting as appendages.

The dramatist suggested that this would be very frightening as a shadow and pulled in the overhead projector to shine their silhouette on the wall. Satisfied with their scary monster, the children posed again and this time the classroom teacher, acting as a lumber company employee, sauntered into the room, examined the shadow, and out loud said: "That's the weirdest thing I've ever seen. Must be shadows from all those trees." As she left the room, the animals gathered again.

The dramatist paused the story and asked them what they were feeling about their efforts to scare off the humans.

Pausing to deepen understanding: What leaving home forever feels like

The children in a multi-age class of students in Grades 1, 2, and 3 were in role as immigrants and having a lot of fun planning what to take with them on a voyage to their new country. They had, in their family groups, packed trunks and boarded the ship, and now they were busy setting up their living space on board. They were definitely "in the play," but the dramatist realized that they did not have any sense of what it meant to leave their home forever.

The dramatist stopped the children's playing and prompted them to reflect on what it would be like if they knew they would never see their home again. After a brief discussion she asked them to think about one thing that they as immigrants would miss from their old home.

The dramatist began to tell their story again, this time describing the scene using some of the dialogue from the children's reflections. Then, when she tapped each child on the shoulder, the child quietly stated what he or she would miss about home: "I will miss my family." "I miss my dog." Children also made comments like: "I don't know what this other place will be like." "I wonder how long it will take before we get there."

Pausing to gather ideas: How to plan a journey to Jupiter

The Kindergarten students were very busy constructing space ships for their voyage to Jupiter. There was a general hum of excitement around the room as they cut windows into their boxes and glued on levers and buttons with an assortment of craft supplies. Every once in a while a child shouted out that he or she had made headlights, a stop button, or a gas tank. Each suggestion was applauded by the adults. The dramatist realized, however, that the children were making these suggestions more as a commentary on their own individual progress rather than as contributions to understanding what might be necessary to have on a space craft.

The dramatist paused their work and brought the children together on the carpet. In this pause the children were able to gather together a long list of requirements for their ships. As their inventory grew, the work on their vessels became more detailed. They began to label their buttons and levers. At this point the classroom teacher made a mental note to find one of astronaut Chris Hadfield's videos of his journey into space so that the children could see inside a real space capsule.

Your Role in the Beginning of Play

Your role is to help the children, through discussion and negotiation, plan a beginning that will bring the whole class together. Achieving this may require a change in the environment and lots of practice as you and the children work to slowly build the dramatic story (see following chapters). You may decide that your class first requires warming up to the idea of playing together. In this case, planning to use drama games such as Sculptor and Clay and Mirrors will be an excellent transition.

You choose the nature of the story's beginning. It may be an action, such as the geese being geese, or it may be a previously established problem or issue, such as animals gathering to confront the loss of habitat.

The open-ended process requires you to take an open stance, listening, observing, being curious about the children's responses, and wondering what will come next. It is important for you to see dramatic play as a step-by-step lived experience. Seldom is this kind of drama played out from beginning to end without discussion, trial and error, reflection, research, and practice.

You prepare the children to be believable within this initial step. You do so by slowing down their desire to take action and laying in the groundwork so that when they do take action, it is believable. Here again, your role is to observe and listen and constantly assess what the next steps might be.

As an observer, you have responsibilities to note student interactions and critically review your practice. The initial stages of the dramatic play experience provide a wonderful opportunity to observe and listen in ways that you may not be able to when a lesson is under way and group work absorbs your focus. During this time you may notice that the dynamics of your classroom shift as children who are often quiet take the lead while others play less prominent parts. This development is nearly always unpredictable.

You will find observing very challenging if you are the only adult in the classroom and you are partnering with the children in their dramatic play. Inviting a parent or teacher assistant to discreetly video while you are involved is an excellent way for you to look back on the experience and examine the process. It will also provide you with insight into classroom dynamics and the interactions between children you may not have noticed as you were playing. If another adult is not available, the next best thing is to find a tripod and set up the camera in an inconspicuous spot with a wide, open lens.

How Dramatic Play Unfolds: Children as Rainforest Creatures

The Rainforest, Part 1

Here is the first of five parts about an exploration of the rainforest by a multi-age class of Grades 1, 2, and 3 students.

The multi-age class was about to begin a unit on the rainforest. The teacher had already gathered books from the library and put up pictures of rainforest flora and fauna, and the children had begun to talk about what they saw. They were, as she predicted, very interested in the creatures. She gave them lots of time to look at the books before she invited them to choose a creature to study. They gathered information over the next few days, drawing, researching on the Internet, checking out books in the library, and putting pertinent information into their own rainforest books.

Before they began their lived-through experience, the classroom teacher asked the students what they might need in order to believe that they were animals in a rainforest. There was much discussion. The children unanimously agreed that they needed trees, vines, and flowers. One child showed the others a picture she had found in one of the books. "Like this," she said, pointing to a tall Kapok tree loaded with vines, monkeys, and parrots. Creating an environment in which the play experience would be believable was the first big step for this dramatic play.

Trees, flowers, and vines that the children made out of carpet rolls, as well as leaves of trees, which the students had painted on large sheets of paper, transformed the classroom. The children's enthusiasm grew along with their rainforest.

Trial transformations

On the day the story was to begin, the dramatist gathered the children in an open area and asked them to each find a space in which they could work without getting in anyone else's way. To assess their willingness to suspend their disbelief, she invited the children to slowly transform into their animal selves from their feet to their heads. This process took several attempts, but taking the time to be believable was important if the children were to play authentically within the story.

Their first practice was chaotic. The monkeys leapt up and down, just missing the cobra that was attempting to slither over the carpet, and the parrots squawked with an ear-shattering squawk. The dramatist asked them to freeze and check in with their bodies to see whether they looked and felt like their animals from their heads to their toes. They started transforming again, and this time she asked them to move in slow motion, checking to see whether they were believable as they moved. She side-coached to remind them of their paws, wings, beaks, and so on. This was the first step.

The first few practices generated much enthusiasm and energy. Assessing their focus and willingness to suspend their disbelief, the dramatist gathered the children on the carpet, and in this pause they discussed what it felt like to be transformed, what they found difficult, and what they would need to be even more believable next time. She invited them to tell each other about their animal and how they thought they might be together in the rainforest — where they might live, who they might be frightened of, what they might eat, thinking that this might be the next step.

At this point no one knew what the story would be about!

SUMMARY
- Have the children practice using stillness and slow motion even before you begin the story.
- With the children, plan a beginning that will engage the whole class and include yourself.
- Practice the willing suspension of disbelief with the children.
- Take small, incremental steps. Consider what is next.
- Stay open to possibilities suggested by the children, and be willing to try them.
- If possible, legitimize children's responses within the story.
- Observe the children carefully.
- Stop and start to pause for discussion, understanding, and research.

---

3 The Importance of Practice

"Although all children are creative, the potential to create remains dormant without practice. With practice, the potential to create becomes a reality."
— Jill Englebright Fox and Robert Schirrmacher, *Art and Creative Development for Young Children,* 8th edition (p. 7)

The Mean Queen   The multi-age class of Grades 1, 2, and 3 students were well into their dramatic play story about a queen who made them as villagers work too hard. Several of the villagers had already been taken to the dungeon (under a table, where they were delighted to be) because they had defied the queen and slept in. The remaining villagers devised a plot to release the prisoners at night.

The dramatist, however, was concerned that, with their heightened enthusiasm and eagerness to act, they were on the brink of chaos. Posing as a sleepy guard, she invited several of the villagers to sneak by the guard and unlock the dungeon door. Between the cheering on of their companions and the *very* noisy approach of the would-be rescuers, the guard awoke each time, and the children as villagers scampered away, barely escaping the guard's sword (a metre stick).

Obviously, the notion of stealth needed to be practiced before the group could continue.

Although dramatic play does not aim for perfection, practice does play a major role. One of the biggest mistakes we can make in any kind of open-ended dramatic experience is to begin at the highest point of action: it is essential to lay the groundwork necessary for the action to be believable, and that requires practice. If you ask Grade 1 students to be wild animals, it is guaranteed that they will have lots of fun, but they may also go out of control, and, no doubt, you will vow never to do drama again! So, practice is not intended to make perfect but to enable the class to act in a way that is appropriate to the scene.

Slowing down the dramatic play is extremely important. Because drama is about the willing suspension of disbelief and seeking to be believable as a participant, it is important that children practice who they are in their dramatic play experience. It is in the practice period that children are invited to plan their character, think about next steps, and organize their actions together. Slowing down also gives children time to develop skills in communicating through voice and movement as they practice, and this practice period provides the teacher with an initial assessment of the children in terms of their commitment to the lived-through experience, their ability to imagine, their skill level and knowledge of the theme, and their ability to work together.

Practice, however, should never impede the momentum of the story or make the experience difficult. This is where your observations as you play with the children become important: you can assess how well the children's energy and enthusiasm keep the story running smoothly or whether their energies are devolving into chaos, which distracts from the initial story idea.

Working towards Focus and Control

Small steps may begin long before the actual dramatic play experience gets under way. As a teacher, you will be aware that any changes in the classroom can be disruptive. Children may not be accustomed to moving around the room or even gathering in a different space or using the space in a different way. They often need practice just to move from their usual seating to another spot in the classroom or in the school where dramatic play might take place. Practicing this transition is important for a smooth beginning. As affirmed earlier, using a drumbeat, for example, can help signal that they are now entering the realm of dramatic play and that a different way of learning is about to occur. Having practiced moving from one point to another will make this transition to play go smoothly.

Taking small steps in planning and practicing is central to children learning about physical control as well. Much like the learning children might do in the gym on the balance beam or ropes, or when kicking or throwing a ball, dramatic play requires physical control. The physical knowing that children experience in play deeply affects their understanding.

In *Into the Story*, Carole Miller and Juliana Saxton (2004, 2) write: "It is their physical engagement offered through the medium of drama — the taking on of a role in imagined situations — that connects and mediates affective and cognitive understandings and deepens students' recognition of who they are in relation to others in a community of learners."

Dramatic play borrows physicality from the theatre world. Most drama curricula will list the skills a child can learn to develop. As in any learning situation, these skills become the means by which children grow in their ability to comprehend, personalize, interpret, and empathize, and become better at collaborating with others.

Most curricula identify dramatic skills in much the following manner:

Use voice, dialogue, body and movement selectively to establish characters and roles and to express feelings.
Collaborate with others in the interpretation of characters.
Sustain a willing suspension of disbelief by staying focused and in character in play experiences. (Manitoba Education 2011)

In an early years classroom, focus and control will look very different than in a senior-high theatre class, however. A theatre class will work at refining these skills in order to clearly communicate their characters within a script or improvisation. In the early years classroom, the children are playing together not so much as individual characters needing to communicate but to work together as a group to establish a story. Body movement and expression of feelings may be necessary to explore and refine, but the willing suspension of disbelief and the ability to stay in the story will be key. Be sure to remember that your class is taking part in play, not performance.

Nonetheless, you will need to constantly assess the worthiness of children's focus in the story. You can do so by asking yourself whether their actions are genuine or whether further practice might give the children more support in what they are doing. If their actions are wild, as were those of the children in the prisoner release scene (see page 29), practice will be required. In another part of the same dramatic play experience, however, insisting on practice would have proved counterproductive.

How to assess potato peeling

When the children in the mean queen story went to work for the queen, their play space was specific while their actions were general. The two girls who worked in the queen's kitchen, for example, always used the same space in front of the windows. No one else used this space. Their play actions were not specific to miming the peeling of potatoes; instead, they made general hand movements that satisfied their role as kitchen help. Likewise, the boys working in the diamond mine made general chopping motions and one boy used a chair as a wheelbarrow, but the mine was always located along the bookshelf.

As adults, we may find it tempting to instruct these movements in order to ensure accuracy and believability. Because this is play, however, there is little need to stop the playing and rehearse the specifics of peeling potatoes or swinging a pick — mimed accuracy is not the point.

Physical Games and Activities to Promote Focus

Playing games that require physical actions and feelings can help children build their expressive capacity in play. For some children, showing expressive capacity will be natural; for others, the idea of using their bodies, voices, and movement will be completely new. Remember, though, that performance is not the end goal of dramatic play; rather, the process is the primary vehicle for learning. If you or your students are new to dramatic play activity, consider the use of stillness or Freeze Frame, as suggested in Chapter 2, as a small step towards a more active play experience. You can also use "freezing" as a way to stop the action during dramatic play to pause, discuss, or refocus.

Especially with students in Grades 4 and 5, establishing a game as a way of entering into dramatic play can be a valuable routine to signal that learning in a different form is about to take place. Games are excellent segues into more complex dramatic play expressions.

Statues

Playing Statues is an opportunity to explore the expressive nature of position, gesture, gaze, and expression, particularly if children are struggling with the physical aspects of who they are in the story. Keeping still is difficult for five- and six-year-olds, but it can also be a skill that they develop over time. In this simple game the child is required to become a statue, perhaps depicting an emotion, such as delight; someone of a certain social status, perhaps a king or a slave; or a particular creature, for example, a mouse or a stork.

There are a few different ways of playing Statues. Children can work in pairs, one as sculptor and the other as clay. Once partners have agreed on what they are depicting, the sculptor either physically or verbally shapes the clay — working verbally provides an opportunity to give specific directions and describe positions. Another approach is to have half the class create statues while the other half does a gallery walk around them. There is a built-in self-regulation as children's efforts are examined by their peers.

Tableaux

Tableaux provide another way to take a small step towards focus and control in dramatic play. A tableau is a "freeze frame" picture. It works well as an introduction to dramatic activity in the classroom because action is expressed in stillness, perhaps with photographs, illustrations, or art reproductions used as references, or as the children's own depiction of a part of the dramatic story.

Tableaux are also useful in exploring complex sections of a story that might be difficult to visualize. For example, where is everyone when the pig gets out in *Charlotte's Web*? Where is Lurvy? Where is the goose? And how do each of the characters look in this particular crisis on the farm? A tableau requires an attention to detail and a genuine understanding that we communicate with much more than words.

Tableaux help children slow down the action when necessary, giving them time to pay attention to how they can physically express emotion and attitude. The children may want to rush into an action at the beginning of the story, but introducing tableaux to practice what that action might look like allows them to explore possibilities that can perhaps be inserted in the story later.

The first step for a tableau experience is for you to find pictures showing people who may or may not be interacting with one another or a short excerpt from a text concerning several people. There needs to be the same number of children in the tableau as represented in a picture or text. Because making a tableau is a visual activity involving groups of children looking at and either re-creating pictures bodily or representing word images concretely, it is helpful if one child in the group is designated the director. This student plays a key role in helping the other group members get into appropriate position.

The following are the elements of tableaux that will support student focus:
- the distance between people — close, touching, too close, far apart
- the direction of a person's gaze — looking at each other, looking away, some looking at others, some not
- the position of the body — standing, on their knees, on a chair, running, expressing a feeling (e.g., fear, shame, anger)
- hand and arm gestures — hands open or clenched, arms raised, reaching out, arms crossed over chest, conveying frustration, anger, pleading
- the tilt of the head — looking down, away, upward, at someone or something
- the position of the legs — astride, bent, aggressive, moving away, moving inward
- tension in the body — tight and controlled, relaxed
- facial expression — showing a particular feeling (e.g., a smile for happiness, knit brows for worry)

One of the best ways to use tableaux with students in Grades 3 and up is to first work with the whole class. Pause the dramatic story, and tell the students that they will be working in groups to establish an interpretation through stillness of what the event, relationships between the characters in their story, or the

You may know a famous Renoir painting of people who have gathered for an afternoon by the river. The painting demonstrates the subtleties of stillness in the telling of a story. As in any image involving people, looking at hands, tilt of head, eye contact, and physical positioning can contribute to understanding who the people might be. A change in any of these positions changes the story. For example, in the Renoir painting, a woman is leaning on her elbow by the railing: she might decide to join the group around the table.

depiction of a particular scene would look like. Before they do so, you can provide a demonstration of the process. Call for willing volunteers to compose a tableau and engage the class in positioning them and discussing tableau ideas. Through the whole-class discussion, for example, students may come to appreciate that there is a big difference in what is communicated between a character standing with open arms and holding himself stiff with crossed arms. This kind of large-group discussion can become interesting as students begin to understand how quickly meaning can change with the alteration of any of the tableau elements. Students then form small groups to work on their own interpretations.

Once the main picture is established, prompt students to imagine and create the next frame or the frame before. When a movement sequence is created in slow motion, students become aware of how the dramatic story can be articulated physically. Using a drumbeat (or tambourine) to sequence the movement from one frame to the next creates a rhythm for the shift in scene. For example, the dramatic story may begin with a bullying scene. The students in small groups establish what they think this scene should look like as a tableau. Once those scenes are established, you can prompt each group to create the scene that comes before and the scene that follows. The children can make before, during, and after bullying-incident tableaux as a drum beats.

Drawing as an Exercise in Sustained Observation

Drawing should not be overlooked during the practice period or during times within dramatic play that might require more reflection and more specific information. Drawing is a way for children to focus their attention and sustain their focus as they gather details and fill in the information necessary to "get the picture." Like physical practice, drawing serves to slow down the process to permit the gathering of more information that will enrich the play experience. A sustained observation of an object can serve as a clarification of part of the story. Looking at and drawing a steamer trunk, for example, gives children time to think about what they might take on a journey to the New World. Sketching pictures of the metamorphosis of a butterfly gives children time to absorb how they might make their own dramatic transformations into butterflies. Seeing how a butterfly's wings are spread and noticing how the butterfly looks when it is about to emerge from the chrysalis enriches the imagination and permits children to replace what is often a generalized action with a more authentic depiction.

The value of guided looking

Sustained looking is sometimes difficult for children as it involves patience and careful observation. It might be necessary to begin the drawing experience with a period of guided looking, during which you visually walk the children through the picture or object, paying close attention to details that would otherwise be missed in a hurried sketch.

For example, in a study of the snowy owl, before the children opened their sketch books, the teacher invited them to silently look at a stuffed owl while she turned it around slowly — they could see it from all angles. She began the guided looking by calling the children's attention to the details of the bird: the shape of the eyes; the pupils, where they were positioned; the delicate patterns of the feathers; the different shapes of the feathers. Once in a while, she paused

Student illustration from a Grade 4 owl study

to ask the children what they noticed. She then continued on until they had fully absorbed as much of the owl's presence as possible.

Teaching children to look carefully and to look often is an important feature of drawing. Look-draws can become a regular experience in the classroom for any significant study whether it be animals, plants, structures, persons, or environments. Certainly, looking and drawing can heighten the dramatic play experience by helping to create a clear picture in the imagination.

Side-Coaching

In side-coaching the teacher co-imagines with the children by describing aloud the *who, what, where,* and *when* of their emerging story. This activity is a key feature of the initial practice period because it gives children time to build their own believability, focus, and control. It also gives you time to assess the children's depth of commitment and focus.

Beginning with the smallest action is a way for children to stay in control and to have a sense of the building blocks required to interpret their role in the play experience. You could, for example, simply ask the children to stand on the spot by their tables as you describe a step-by-step transformation into character and the children respond. If they are being animals, the children may have already practiced by drawing their animal or they may have a picture of their animal to look at. You might ask them to close their eyes and visualize what they are to become.

The next step is a slow transformation as they listen to being side-coached into role from their feet through to their heads, exploring just how their animal might look. For example, if the children are playing the role of animals, you would have them think about their feet. Are they on their toes? Are their toes pointed in or out? Are they best on all fours, standing, or crouching? And how are their arms positioned? What about their head and eyes? Can they feel their feet turning into paws? It is impossible to be exactly as the animal is, of course, but this exercise is intended to slow down the action of leaping about as a monkey, for example, so that the children will gain a clearer picture of the animal in their imaginations.

Like the look-draw activity, you are assisting them in developing their practice through active visualization.

Side-coaching becomes part of the storytelling process and often serves as the repeated link from one day to the next. In the animal scenario, for example, the teacher might begin the story with the animals asleep in their homes around the classroom. (See "How Dramatic Play Unfolds: Creatures gather in the rainforest," at the end of the chapter.) Giving children time to find the appropriate place is important. It is lots of fun for bears to crawl under a table and birds to each find the right chair for a perch. Circulating among "the animals" as they settle into their new-found spaces, you can identify each of them as a particular animal and describe their sleeping areas, thereby deepening the imaginative journey. Again, the children may require a bit of practice since curling up under a table for the first time is very exciting.

Once the children as animals are in position in their imaginary homes, the teacher, in best storytelling voice, begins speaking: *"The animals huddled snug in their dens and on their perches. From time to time, they peeked out to see if the human was still there. It did not feel safe, not until night fell. Then they slowly and cautiously crept from the safety of their homes to gather on the shore to talk."* By side-coaching through narration, the teacher sets the mood through which the children respond. When they return to the story next, children often request that the story begin in exactly the same place with exactly the same words.

Action is, of course, the primary goal of dramatic play. It is the most fun for children — and rather scary for adults. Depending on the story, however, action may not always mean high physical action. It may simply be feeling the tension of a particular situation. The point of practice is to give the children time to get into character and to act in a way that is focused and believable.

Any attempts to make children as animals stand upright are much more about adult need for control than the children's sense of authenticity and play. Such attempts will also be futile. Although you might want the children standing by their desks to wriggle like a boa constrictor as you demonstrate, it is inevitable that boa constrictors and other reptiles must be on their bellies on the floor and that four-legged creatures will need to be on all fours.

A tiger on all fours

Slow Motion Practice

Most children understand the convention of slow motion. When there is need for high action or physical combat in a story, you will want to practice slow motion before they begin the fight, as a way of controlling the action in a safe and focused manner. Any sword fighting, fleeing, or scrambling up a mountain can be executed in fine detail when done in "slow mo.' " In fact, the scene is more fun to do and watch when it unfolds in slow motion. Your role as dramatist is to help students choreograph the action as they work out the details of moving *veeerryy* slowly!

An illustration of when to use slow motion: A sword fight

A group of boys is working on a skit that they have agreed to do on their own as part of a larger story. They are planning a sword fight between the prince's warriors and the villain. They have already asked if they can bring in plastic swords from home, but you have insisted that they make cardboard swords at school.

Before they begin the sword fight, you realize that they need support and practice so you spend time with them choreographing their moves in slow motion, as happens in the movies. For example, as one warrior raises his sword, the villain blocks it with his. The villain may then slowly turn and raise his sword to block another warrior coming from behind. If actions are organized in slow motion like a dance, the boys will be able to create a fight scene that looks and feels authentic.

Carefully, you work out with the boys the beginning, middle, and end of their sword fight. All in slow motion, the scene demands much energy and concentration for the boys to stay focused, remember the choreography, and complete the scene. They rehearse the fight until it is perfect.

Your Role during Practice

Strive to stay open to new ideas during the initial practice period. This time informs the way in which the play might unfold, but it also allows the children to explore multiple approaches. Working by trial and error, having discussions, generating ideas, and trying things out are just as important in dramatic play as they are to any learning situation. Children need time to explore their characters, adopt different points of view, share ideas, and discuss whether or not they are believable.

Do your best to ensure that the pre-play practice experience supports the children's ideas and provides an opportunity for you to see a wide range of related possibilities. This is really the pleasure of working within play; you, with the children, can flexibly move around a scenario to explore multiple interpretations and other points of view. There may be many ways for a monkey to enter the clearing in the jungle, for example. Children can play villagers complaining about their king; they can also be courtiers in the palace complaining about the villagers. Both kinds of roles are worthy of attention and can offer students a great deal of insight. Lower-status roles can give children insight into oppression and frustration as well as into problem solving and empowerment; higher-status roles give them a chance to consider power and privilege but also to understand how exercise of these can bring about positive change, such as reconciliation and justice.

Trying several possibilities expands a child's imaginative capacity and positions you as the teacher as the one who is curious rather than as the one who knows with a single approach.

Neutral and curious

Because dramatic play is rooted in the creative process, you will need to remain as neutral and as curious about the children's thinking as possible throughout the practice and play making. Doing so will allow a range of imaginative possibilities to be revealed. The temptation is for the adult to demonstrate, correct, and tell children what to do, but do not yield to it. You may find yourself making the monkey's movements only to discover that most of the troop of monkeys mimic exactly what you have done. Yet allowing the child to discover a unique interpretation through exploring often feels like it will lead to chaos. Dramatic play, however, is about connecting with the imagination and recognizing that children have the capacity to interpret as well as focus their ideas with practice if we but take the time to prepare them.

How Dramatic Play Unfolds: Practicing Their Way into Character

Two authentic dramatic play experiences offer examples of building a story through practice in getting into character and moving into position. "Meeting on Mt. Olympus" includes a problem-solving meeting of Greek gods; "Creatures gather in the rainforest" focuses on students becoming believable as rainforest creatures.

Meeting on Mt. Olympus

Greek Gods

This first example of building story through practice involves a class of students in Grades 1, 2, and 3.

A multi-age class had been studying various characters in Greek mythology. Students had each chosen a character to be and had thoroughly studied the character's history, read related storybooks, drawn pictures, and generally immersed themselves in the mythology. The dramatist invited them to play together as their Greek characters and asked if they would like to gather as a group to solve a problem. They agreed, and when she asked them how they wanted to begin their story, they appropriately suggested that they be called to a meeting by the child who had studied Zeus.

Before the action began, however, one child showed the class a picture of the gates of Olympus, the entrance into the court of Zeus. The children decided that they must first construct a representation of the gates.

The next day the dramatist called the children to the carpet and while they stood on the spot, she coached them into their characters, from toes to heads. She watched, carefully reminding them to each build a character that would be believable. They practiced several times and when they were all satisfied that they had adequately interpreted who they were, she asked them to find a place in the classroom that would be their home. Several children erected the gates while the rest of the class rushed off to their places in the classroom. Zeus, of course, stood on a chair and snapped together some markers to make a lightning bolt. Having practiced his role beforehand and read stories about his character, the student was prepared to assume his key part.

When the children had all found their places, the dramatist circulated among them. She mentioned each character by name, using words similar to those on a chart about the characters that she and the children had compiled the day before. She noted to herself that they seemed to be taking this experience quite seriously although there had been some argument over whose space was whose.

Aware of the value of taking small steps in planning, the dramatist paused the story to ask the children *how* Zeus should call them to their meeting and what the problem to address might be. They decided that Zeus should ring a bell (it was nearby), and after some discussion they agreed that the problem should be with the humans. The dramatist was open to what the problem with the humans might be, while realizing that this session would be full of complaints! Zeus rang the bell — and immediately several of the boys pushed and shoved their way onto the carpet, bypassing the gates.

The dramatist paused the group and asked for suggestions on how the characters would enter into the court of Zeus. After a brief discussion and a few demonstrations by individual children, members of the class returned to their places and on cue made their approach again. After the third practice they were satisfied that they felt "in character" and ready to begin their story.

The student in role as Zeus again rang the bell. This time the other students solemnly entered in character through the gates of Mount Olympus, and Zeus, well aware of his power, listened as they described their problems with the humans. Some of the issues raised were silly, but the dramatist, not wanting to lose momentum at this point, let them go, knowing that eventually these children would come up with viable ideas.

The children as gods continued with their complaints until one character stated that the humans were destroying all of the trees. The dramatist recognized this as an excellent foundation for the rest of the story. She stopped the action and asked the gods whether this crisis might be a legitimate one for them to deal with. They thought it might, and the children returned to the story to discuss in character what destroying all the trees would mean and how they might stop this trend on Earth.

Creatures gather in the rainforest

The Rainforest, Part 2

This description continues the dramatic play experience of children in a multi-age class of Grades 1, 2, and 3 students exploring the rainforest.

The children had practiced transforming into their creatures while standing on the spot, and the dramatist felt convinced that most of them could stay focused and were ready to participate in a lived-through experience. The class had a good discussion about who they were as animals or insects, and the three boys who were jungle cats stopped chewing on the monkey's shoulders! The cobras, panthers, spiders, butterflies, monkeys, and bees did well at being believable within the rainforest environment.

The dramatist did not yet know what the story would be about, but she did know that the next step was to bring everyone together in a genuine play experience and that she, too, would need to play a role. The dramatist chose the sloth as her animal, and the children informed her in detail how a sloth would be.

Concerned that the library was a new and fairly large space in which to play, the dramatist decided to beat a drum to call the children together. Before that, though, the children as creatures each had to find a place in the room that would be home. Directing the children to do this felt a bit risky to the classroom teacher, who was observing and documenting the experience, but she quickly noted that the children found it exciting to determine a home. They loved snuggling into places where they would not normally be allowed to go, and the library afforded a number of attractive possibilities. They were completely on task.

"*Look around the space,*" prompted the dramatist, "*and see if there is a place where you might like to be as your animal or insect.*"

When the dramatist asked them to move, there was initial chaos — this is to be expected. The children were eager to find their places so she let them go and circulated through the space, commenting and side-coaching at each station. "*Ah yes, the butterflies are resting near their favorite flowers.*" (The two girls stood on chairs on either side of a big flower the children had made to decorate their play space in the library.) "*And I see that the monkeys have gathered together as usual . . .*" (Three boys crouched on a table.) The boy who was a bee had found an open shelf on the floor and was snuggled inside, pleased with his find. The rest of the class settled in under tables, behind shelves, and within a barricade of chairs.

Having established a "clearing" and a drumbeat signal with the dramatist ahead of time, the children huddled in their hiding places and listened for the drum to call them together. The dramatist waited for them to settle and then began the drumbeat. On cue the children burst out of their hiding places and rushed to the carpet. The monkeys slid into place — they were all very much out of character.

"*I didn't believe you,*" the dramatist reported. "*We will have to practice this again so that* you *can really believe that you are animals.*"

On the spot, the children practiced transforming again, working from toes to head, and then the dramatist invited them to return as their creatures to their hiding places. This time, when the drumbeat summoned the creatures, the arrivals were more focused. The children practiced several times, more coming and going from their places of hiding to the clearing in the forest.

Practicing on the spot

Focus on this dramatic play experience continues in Chapter 4.

The final time the children returned to their places, the dramatist asked them to be silent — the story was about to begin. Using a storytelling voice, she began: *"It was nightfall in the rainforest, and all the creatures were safe and sound in their places. The monkeys were in the trees. The butterflies were snuggled under a leaf. The cobras were tucked under a log, and the panthers were stretched out asleep on a log..."*

Quiet enveloped the group as the children listened. The dramatist continued speaking: *"The sun began to slowly rise, its rays penetrating the canopy and waking the animals."* She noticed several children stretching and yawning and considered this a true test of living in the story. *"It was then that they heard the drum..."* Without any coaching, the children silently began their journey to the clearing. They were now believable as the animals they had practiced to be.

SUMMARY

- Use strategic drama games and activities to set the tone and practice focus, control, and expression.
- Move from stillness, taking small steps to more and more action.
- Practice being believable characters before you and the children begin constructing the story.
- Side-coach to set the tone of the experience.
- Use slow motion to control the action.
- Invite children to create the space, and practice using the space.
- Stay open to possibilities for interpretation through discussion and trial and error.
- Have students practice coming to the gathering space or being in an individual space in character.
- Use drawing to slow down the play process and enrich the imagination.
- Remember that playfulness and fun are central to dramatic play.

4 Building Belief

> "Drama, like story, is judged by the degree to which it is believable or true to human experience. This does not mean that a group of students might not decide to create an impossible fantasy world, but once it is decided upon, the action and intentions of the actors in that world must be believable."
> — Betty Jane Wagner, *Educational Drama and Language Arts* (p. 28)

All dramatic processes require both a willing suspension of disbelief and an active effort to promote believability. Children entering into imaginative play may need to explore a variety of ways to build belief in order to participate fully in the unfolding story. You want them to believe who they are at the beginning of the story — and practice plays an important role in fostering this. Because they have an opportunity for play, most children eagerly establish a believable scenario, but it may not be exactly as you imagined.

Balancing Play Energy and Theatre Practice

Teachers may want a more theatrical play experience and so be tempted to interrupt the dramatic playing in order to focus on skills. As noted in Chapter 3, though, doing so would be counterproductive. We have all likely observed kitchen play where the cook quickly stirs an imaginative pot and dumps the contents onto an imaginary plate. It is not important that the child mime exactly how a pot is stirred or its contents ladled onto a plate in order for the child to *believe* he is in the kitchen cooking. Practice and belief do go hand in hand, but neither should take over the momentum and excitement of pretending. You will be obliged to engage in much ongoing reflection to weigh the value of play energy over the development of theatrical details.

Remember that dramatic play is not a linear process, and so pausing, discussing possibilities and next steps, practicing, and building belief become important companions for children playing and exploring together. Stopping the momentum of play in order to plan the next steps or reflect on possibilities or difficulties that emerge can be hard to do, however. Using a signal can help to indicate a shift from being in the dramatic play to emerging from it. These shifts can be moment by moment, step by step as you co-construct next moves with the children.

Pausing to reflect or discuss next steps does not seem to hinder dramatic play. Children move fluidly back and forth from group decisions and suggestions to playing in the story. Each phase of the story may require practice and building belief much as the work of a writer or artist may be subject to continual editing, reworking, and review of the integrity of the process. This incremental approach, whereby the dramatic story unfolds slowly amid the asking of questions, sharing of ideas, and talk of possibilities, places dramatic play in the unique position of engaging children together in thoughtful planning that holds dramatic tension and story at the same time.

At the beginning of the story, it is crucial that you take the time to build belief. Practice is important but once the students are satisfied with their initial entrance as characters into the story, other strategies can be used to take them further in their exploration.

Using Space to Help Suspend Disbelief

The beginning point of a dramatic play story often occurs as the people or animals (mythic or otherwise) gather in a particular environment. This meeting is a natural part of the play experience. Children can spend much more time setting up the play house, the veterinary clinic, or the fort than they do playing in the space. You probably remember spending childhood hours bunching up leaves to create a specific environment only to have them all blow away. The fun was not so much in playing in the space but rather in discussing, agreeing and disagreeing, and searching for the right things to use to create the perfect environment.

It is important that you negotiate use of the play area for the characters with the children and give them lots of opportunity to set up a play space that will help them suspend their disbelief. The space should, of course, reflect what the story requires. For example, the story might call for a trip in an airplane, in which case, seating arrangements are needed. Asking the children to help you set this up is part of the beginning process and very much about building and supporting belief. The story might begin on a train or in a boat, at night, or in a hideout with the lights out. The children will have many suggestions that you can explore with them. The class might try out several ideas until they find the space that works and that supports their willing suspension of disbelief.

In the green of the rainforest

Sometimes, the nature of the space becomes more evident as research and idea generating continue in anticipation of the story not yet begun. Research can lead to the creation of a very specific physical environment. For example, the children immersed in the rainforest study created the canopy of the rainforest. The setting they developed was more elaborate than simply gathering a few objects. Creating trees, vines, and flowers to change the classroom space provided them with an environment for their dramatic play that contributed to the believability of their story. It also served as an expression of what they had learned about rainforest flora.

Avoid using the gym as a setting unless you need a place of high action. It is large and echoes.

This tree is one of several that a multi-age class, Grades 1 to 3, made as part of its rainforest study.

Down in the dungeon

The Fairy Tale, Part 2

The earlier part of this dramatic play experience appears in the Introduction.

The Grade 1 students constructing their very own fairy tale together built their story step by step, each time discussing how to make the next event more believable. When the witch cast her spell and sent them into the dungeon, for example, the story paused so that the children could discuss where their dungeon might be and how they would be in the dungeon.

The dramatist asked, *"What do we need to do to make a dungeon and make it feel like a dungeon when we are in it?"*

The children made the decision to use a corner of the classroom between a bookcase and wall. The space was tiny, but they agreed that it would feel like a dungeon because they would all be crammed in. One child suggested using the chairs to block off the entrance and make it look like bars. Another suggested turning off the lights. Agreeing that this setup would work as their dungeon, the dramatist backed the story up to the point when the witch waved her magic wand and marched them into the dungeon.

At times, children may simply need the lights turned out or a certain place designated in the classroom in order to build their belief in a situation.

The story then began again . . .

Practicing within the space

Practice within a specific setting takes on a new energy. Despite that positive feature, you may find that the initial practice is chaotic as the children enthusiastically rush to their created spaces. You will need patience and perseverance to get past this. Taking the position of observer, giving the children feedback, and discussing the believability of the first practice are important. This discussion becomes an opportunity for the children to share their perceptions and try out some new ideas together. They may need to practice "on the spot" again until you and they are satisfied that their actions are believable.

Using Narration to Cast a Spell

One way to build belief in dramatic play is to borrow from storytelling. When we tell stories, we use a special storytelling voice that sets the atmosphere. You have probably observed what happens when you begin a story with more than just a reading voice, that is, when you vary vocal range and volume, adjust your speaking pace, give key words emphasis, pause and look at the children during tense moments, and convey meaning through your face to help create the scene. Children are captivated by the magic spell of the storyteller, and that is exactly what narration does — it casts a spell.

Using this strategy at the beginning of a dramatic play experience or to settle a group after a heightened play period is effective, but it also works well when the story is progressing over several days. The children often demand that they begin in exactly the same place physically and with exactly the same opening words to the story they are living through. *"Once upon a time long, long ago, in a castle far away . . ."* already begins to weave a spell as the children, in their starting places, wait to be brought into action.

If you are comfortable thinking quickly, the narration can also be spontaneous, provided that you use a storytelling voice that creates the atmosphere required. Narrating slows down the action and supports getting into character while cueing the students for what actions need to be taken.

An example of narration

"As night faded, the sun began to peek above the horizon and all the animals in the forest began to wake. [This statement tells the children where they are and what is happening.] *Slowly, slowly, they stretched and yawned.* [The children hear some actions they might use and are reminded to do them slowly.] *It was then that they heard the drum.* [The drum is something previously discussed and perhaps rehearsed.] *They remembered that this was the signal for them to gather in the clearing. As the drum beat, the animals, one by one, began moving into the clearing.* [Again, the narrator's words signal what their action will be.] *The wolf crept silently, the garter snake slithered . . ."* [Each animal is cued in terms of a possible action, or their action cues the narration.]

This narration not only sets the tone, but also helps to build belief.

Using Rumors to Promote Imagining

Working with rumors is a strategy that helps children imagine the complexities of their dramatic circumstance. This approach works best when the class engaged in dramatic play is in a difficult situation that may require escape or negotiation. Rumors serve to build the case of what they are up against in their story. For example, perhaps the children are creating a story about a despot king. In that case, the question *"What have you heard about the King?"* is all that is necessary to begin building a believable story in which the children's imagined personal experience is foremost. Listening to and accepting all rumors regardless of their value in the story is important to staying in the story. A rumor, after all, is just that — a rumor.

Tapping In: Towards a Deeper Level

Tapping In is a reflective strategy that builds belief and often takes the dramatic story to a deeper emotional level. Carole Miller and Juliana Saxton describe this method in *Into the Story*: "The teacher moves through the group placing a hand on each participant's shoulder and asking a question such as, 'Tell me what you are thinking.' 'What are your concerns?'" (2004, 160).

Use of this strategy is most effective during times in the dramatic story that call for a more personal reflective response. For example, the participant is on a boat leaving the familiar for the unknown, is captured and locked up, is lost in the wilderness, or is contemplating a disaster.

Tapping In very naturally creates a quiet mood that can lead directly into writing in role (see page 48).

Using Research to Provide Detail

Once the story has begun you may want the children to deepen their understanding by "filling in the picture." Doing this may require much stopping and starting to check in, plan, and examine ideas in order to create a more believable experience. Often, the children are aware of what needs to be filled in, but you will want to encourage them to develop the imaginative picture further. Filling in becomes an important part of building belief as it slows down the action and works between the lines to develop details and provide the research necessary to create a believable story. Children seek more information enthusiastically when they are living through the story.

Impetus to learn: Getting ready for a recruiter

The Crew of *La Grande Hermine*, Part 1

This dramatic play experience is further discussed in Chapter 6: Playing inside Curriculum.

In all of the classroom experiences presented thus far, you will notice that there comes a point before or during the dramatic play experience when more information is required. The children engaged in the rainforest, fairy-tale, and Greek god stories had all studied the basic information necessary for their stories to begin with some authenticity. When the dramatist, in role as a recruiter for Jacques Cartier's voyage to the New World, met with a Grade 4/5 class, however, the intention of the play experience was different: it was to send the children deeper into understanding the life on board a ship in the sixteenth century.

The children had begun their study of this time period but had only a basic understanding. Their knowledge had not yet moved from the cursory factual to a visceral felt sense of what life might have been like. After the first encounter with the recruiter, the students felt the necessity to find out more, and this effort became part of the imagined journey on board *La Grande Hermine*. The desire to learn more about ships and jobs on board them was a palpable energy, and the week that followed saw a flurry of activity as the Grades 4/5 class enthusiastically researched the various positions held by crew on board a ship in the sixteenth century. The students learned ship terminology, investigated and selected individual roles, and developed demonstrations of skills to apply to join Cartier's crew when the recruiter returned.

Augmenting Understanding through Art

Icarus makes his wings.

Through simple sketches, costume pieces, props, and masks, students can deepen their understanding of who they are within a dramatic play experience.

Sketching Portraits: Often, students can improve their understanding of a character by quite literally filling in a picture through drawing. Drawing a self-portrait of their character gives time for individual participants to fill in some of the details of who they are in order to "get the picture." Looking at picture books, video clips, and information texts will expand their understanding, particularly if the story leads them out of their range of experience.

Dressing Up: Consider developing a "tickle trunk" for your classroom, so that you have a resource for allowing a student to pose in a costume, perhaps suggestive of period, for portrait drawing. In the trunk you could keep large pieces of cloth, various plastic hats, cardboard tubes, and perhaps objects that hint at certain historical periods, for example, a candle, a parasol, an apron, a sack, and a jewellery box.

Producing Props: Making props can be important to the story. Props can also provide an expanded learning experience in art as well as in other curricular areas. For example, in the picture at left, a Grade 3 student is about to take part in the final chapter of the class's story of Icarus. He is on the verge of finishing his wings. This art experience was the culmination of a study of bird wings and wing feathers, measurement, and problem solving in terms of how to fasten the wings on the arms. Doing all of this enhanced the believability of the story's finale as the children flew away from their prison in the tower, which was in the gym.

Art activities may also lead to other kinds of construction representing set pieces. Building a spacecraft or space console out of a cardboard box may aid children in playing fully and believably while they are in their story.

Making Masks: Creating masks — especially for animals — is another way of building belief through sketching, research, and planning. Below are images of plaster-strip masks. Children each researched an animal and chose the material to cover their mask from a variety of fabrics.

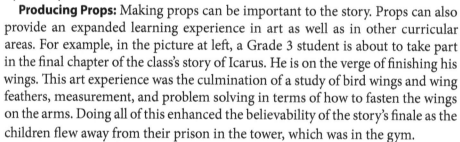

Tree frog, woolly monkey, and jaguar masks

Building Belief through Use of Blank Paper

Although it may sound improbable, one of the best ways to build belief and begin the story is to use a blank piece of flip-chart paper and a marker. There is something magical about this as the children gather on the carpet and you draw something that may look like a river, a forest, mountains, or a lake depending on the story. If you begin by saying something like, *"I know that there is a mountain range here, but I forget where we are in relation to it,"* inevitably, a child will point to a place on the paper where the group is located. Thus, the story begins with specifics. Other children begin to add to the map. They point out more details not previously discussed so that the group will know where — and sometimes what — dangers or challenges are to be faced.

Building belief with blank paper

In dramatic play about regaining a castle (see How Dramatic Play Unfolds, pages 15 to 17), the story's beginning came into focus when a blank sheet of paper was shown. To begin, the dramatist simply drew a wobbly line, suggesting a river, and asked where their hideout might be. The group went on to locate the castle and identify other landmarks that could be important to the story. For children, the imagination can color-in details, even on a largely blank sheet of paper with just a wobbly line, a circle, or an *X* marking the spot.

This approach is a delightful way in which to begin a very open-ended story, but also relevant to use if the children already have some background knowledge and you want them to develop a story together as a group. For example, a Grade 4 class was studying the Cree First Nations before European contact. Students sat around a large blank piece of paper, and the dramatist drew a wavy line indicating a river. She looked at one of the children and asked, *"Where is your teepee?"* Without hesitation the child pointed to the top of the paper, adding that the teepee was near a forest. Thus, the story began with a community establishing itself on an almost empty sheet of chart paper.

Writing in Role and First-Person Singular

When the story has begun it may be necessary for the children to fill in detail through writing a journal in the first-person singular or writing in role. This experience invites them to enter into the backstory of their character in order to build their imagination and deepen their beliefs about who they are and how they are affected by their circumstances.

The backstory can also be enhanced by research. In the example below, the Grade 4 student as pirate has obviously researched some of the vocabulary of a sailor. Her story serves her well as the class enters further into the large-group experience as pirates.

Transcription:

Hey there! I'm going to tell you about how I became a pirate. I remember my old life. It was a tragic life. I had no food, no money, no house, and not even a family. One day I saw a sailor beside a merchant ship. The man looked sad. I walked up to him and said why are you sad. The man said I lost my men in a storm. I thought for a while. Then I said how about I join your crew. The sailor paused for a second. Then he agreed. First I took my first bath in a co[u]ple years. Then he got me in a sailor uniform. After we set a driftd into the high seas. Wyle I was swbing the deck he was very strickt. He said work more hard!!! Wyle I was mending . . .

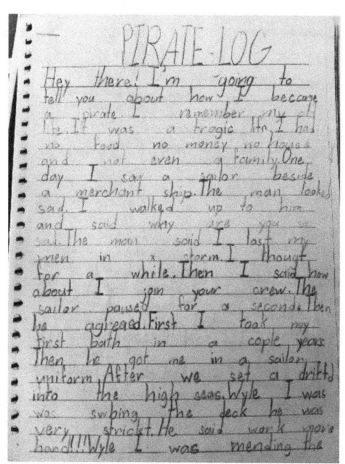

Part of a pirate's log

Writing in role is a thinking tool for children, particularly in the higher grades, enabling them to reflect back on their lived-through experiences. It gives them time to gather their thoughts and add a personal perspective to the group story. Because the story is a lived-through experience demanding the child's imaginative participation, writing in role supports a richer, more dimensional writing than is usually achieved through imagining alone. Writing about what actually happened and how it felt expands children's understanding of story with built-in details, atmosphere, tensions, conversations, and interactions that fuel the children's writing and drawing.

In the story of regaining the castle (see "How Dramatic Play Unfolds" in Chapter 1), the children built a tunnel in the classroom. The teacher later invited them to crawl back into the tunnel to write personal stories in their journals. Because this was a "real" experience full of tension, emotion, and adventure, the children's motivation to tell about their characters' experiences was heightened. Their writing was much more expressive than usual.

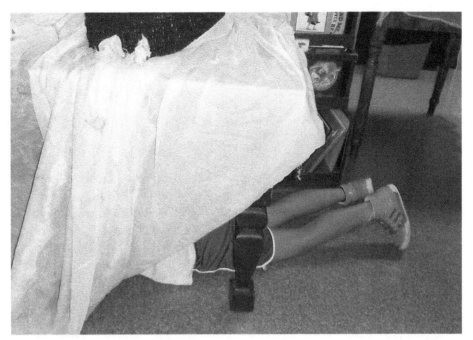

Writing in the castle's secret tunnel

Your Role in Building Belief

Pausing throughout the dramatic play experience to discuss next steps and build belief is one of your major roles as you create a story with the children. You need to determine what will deepen belief while moving the story forward. Do the children need to write in role? Do they need to create a space in more detail? Is there a role you might play to move them further into the story? (See Chapter 7 on teacher in role.) Pausing allows you the time to craft whatever is necessary to further the story with the children.

As the dramatic story progresses, however, you may see the need through your own research to fill in some of the areas that are missing in order to deepen the students' belief. Making masks makes the transformation into animals believable. Creating some kind of badge suggests that the students are part of an organization. Drawing a picture of the castle makes the imagined visible and adds detail to the circumstance. Building belief is a constant spiraling as you move with the children through the story, pausing along the way, reflecting, writing, drawing, and researching in order to develop their understanding. At the beginning, however, all that the children might require are the lights out, some sound effects, or a rearrangement of classroom furniture.

Throughout the story you will find that you ask a wide range of questions of yourself and of the children, for example:

- Do we need to arrange the space for the children to believe that they are in a different setting?
- What do they need to research in order to fill in their understanding of who they are or what their situation is?

As you pause the story, make sure that you stay open to the children's ideas, asking yourself questions like these:

- Does the child's suggestion build belief in the story?
- Does the suggested idea need to be lived through?

- Will the suggestion lead to other possibilities?
- Does the suggestion require more research?
- Does the suggestion move the story in another direction worth pursuing?
- Does the suggestion invite the whole group to participate?

How Dramatic Play Unfolds: Building Belief within a Story

Here are two illustrations of how students developed their belief in a story and in their roles within it. The first dramatic play experience is based on the picture book *The Mitten* by Jan Brett, and the second returns to the rainforest unit, earlier discussed in Chapters 2 and 3. In each of these illustrations, you will notice how the story details emerge from the children and how belief grows as they become invested in the story through practice, pausing, and their own interpretations.

Hiding under a mitten

Animals under the Mitten

The Mitten is a story that all Grade 1 students love. Its ingredients are ideal for them: animals, a large mitten, a sneeze, even a Baba! The story also lends itself to dramatic play.

On the carpet on one occasion, the dramatist asked the children if they would like to participate as animals in *The Mitten*. Of course, they agreed, calling out a wide range of creatures they wanted to be. Since their choices went well beyond the animals featured in the story, she let them be what they wanted. Four boys chose to be bears and began tumbling over one another. It looked like fun, but the dramatist wanted to see whether they could control their tumbling enough to take part with the rest of the group as they played in the familiar story.

The dramatist asked the children to each find a spot on the carpet where they would not bother anyone: they were going to practice being their creature. The butterfly immediately began to open her wings, the turtle curled up in a ball, and the rabbit complained about the difficulty of hopping on the spot! The bears, however, could not get beyond grabbing at each other and roaring.

Not willing to give up, the dramatist called out "freeze," a game the students were familiar with. The children obediently froze into elaborate poses. *"I am going to slowly transform you into your animals from your toes to your head. Do you think you can do it?"* They affirmed that they could and she began, emphasizing each animal's transformation. Several times she reminded the bears that they were working to be believable as bears. Finally, one of them got down on all fours. Progress!

Slowly but surely, after two more practices, the animals came to life.

"Let's test our believability," the dramatist said. *"On your own spot, can you sleep as your creature would sleep? Think about what that would look like, and when you are ready, go ahead and sleep."*

Addressing this small step seemed to enable even the bears to focus as they curled up in an imaginary den. The butterfly asked, "Do butterflies sleep, teacher?" Hmmm. From their sleep, the dramatist side-coached them to eat and then move. By then, they were all in character.

The next step was to introduce the big soft white blanket that the dramatist had brought to represent the mitten. She imagined all the children on cue under it, waiting for the big sneeze. What she did not anticipate was the excitement that ensued when she produced the blanket. When she asked the children whether it would do as a mitten, they reached for it, and before she knew what was happening, they had spread it out and gone under it, giggling with delight.

The dramatist was tempted to put on her teacher voice and abandon the whole experience, but then she realized that this was, indeed, lots of fun. In the spirit of play, she dove under the blanket with the giggling children. She reclaimed the blanket and this time asked the children to practice being their animals and coming under the blanket. One by one they each crawled, flittered, lumbered, or hopped under the blanket where she was, as well.

"Now wait for the sneeze." She teased them a bit, much to their delight, until on cue they gave a big sneeze and all tumbled out.

When the children were ready for the actual story, she gathered them to their places on the carpet from where even the bears took turns slipping under the blanket. The sneeze was successful, and she asked one child to gather up the blanket and pretend to be the boy while she would be Baba. Several students wanted to play the part of the boy and did so, providing a range of interpretations as each of them handed the stretched mitten back.

Drought comes to the rainforest

The Rainforest, Part 3

Here, the multi-age classroom of students in Grades 1, 2, and 3, further explore the rainforest.

The dramatist beat the drum and, as planned, the animals began their journey to the clearing. The classroom teacher had helped the students build believability in their animals through drawings, picture books, their own research booklets, and the creation of rainforest flora for their dramatic play space in the library. Their dramatic practice had settled them into their animal skins, and the dramatist noticed that they were all very credible animals as they slithered, hopped, crawled, and flew to the clearing on the carpet.

The dramatist introduced herself again as Serendipity Sloth and told them that she had heard rumors about a pending disaster. She asked if they were willing to discuss this in a formal council meeting. She invited the children in role to form a circle and told them that each animal, while passing a stick, could say what it feared. She listened as the children, one by one, expressed concerns. Their comments ranged from the personal — "something is stealing my babies" — to broader concerns about feeling frightened at night because of predators. The dramatist affirmed each child's contribution, waiting for the one idea that would extend the story further for the whole group and carry the dramatic play forward.

When the story is not known and is dependent on the suggestions of children, this waiting will feel like a big risk. Without exception, however, children seem able to reach a level of classic understanding of story that brings the potential for a lived-through experience into focus. In this case, the boy who was a bee stated that it had not rained for months and he could not find any nectar because the flowers were all dying. The butterflies were quick to confirm this, and there ensued a discussion, quite unsolicited, about the impact of a drought. The dramatist paused the story and invited the children to say what they knew about droughts.

The students later found information on the impact of drought through some basic research on how drought affected both parts of their country and other countries.

SUMMARY
- Practice and building belief go hand in hand.
- Create a space that reflects the story.
- Narration supports the atmosphere and action of the story.
- Rumors encourage children to build responses to the story's tension.
- *In-filling* refers to the between-the-lines investigation and research whereby children can develop a fuller picture of the story.
- Blank paper can effectively initiate a story.
- Use art and writing in role to deepen story.
- Listen carefully for opportunities that will take the story further.
- Pause and start when necessary in order to discuss, launch more research, and refocus the story.

5 Finding the Story

"Drama and story are closely interlinked. They are not the same thing; but without a strong narrative it is difficult to sustain interest in a drama."
— Brian Woolland, *The Teaching of Drama in the Primary School* (p. 18)

As an early years teacher, you already know that children love responding to stories. They react readily to descriptions, sounds, atmospheres, and characters described by the author as you read aloud. Two children may hug each other when the story reaches a scary climax, several children will howl in response to hearing about a dog baying at the moon, and you will suddenly hear the sound of wind as you talk about a windy day. We have all had the experience of watching a play unfold as a group of children retell a story dramatically, following the storyline, becoming the characters, and developing the dialogue as they remember it. These are all natural responses to story that we experience every day in the classroom. These kinds of responses are also indications that children are already aware of the connections between dramatic play and story.

Story is everywhere. Wherever there are characters, be they human, animal, or even inanimate objects, there are story possibilities. Wherever there is a tension, a happening, or a decision to be made, there is potential for story. There are stories in social studies, in science, in storybooks, and in life itself. We are naturally story people, and children are natural actors when it comes to playing out stories, whether they know the endings or not.

Unlike children playing on their own, in dramatic play, the adult is very present as co-constructor in both the planning and the guiding. The response and much of the direction, however, come from the children. Listening for the story and the learning possibilities as you move with the children is key to a successful dramatic play experience.

Walking with Words: Working with a Story Text

"When we are in drama, it is like walking in the pages of a book. The words do not just lie there; they come alive and walk with us. That makes me want to stay in the drama because I don't want to leave the words behind."
— Beatrice, in Warner (1997)

Stories, of course, lend themselves readily to dramatic play. As previously stated, however, dramatic play functions to deepen the story through *lived-through experiences* with the whole class, rather than simply be a re-enactment of a story. You will need to identify the story areas that might be enriched or clarified through a dramatic play experience. Carole Miller and Juliana Saxton provide the following comment in *Into the Story*:

While not every story, poem, play, novel or article should be explored through drama, experiences in drama promote a literacy that is three-dimensional. Drama makes it possible for students to represent their understandings in a variety of ways that are not available through more traditional methodologies. And when students sit down to read or write, they bring those internalized drama experiences to the little black marks on the page . . . They know for themselves and in themselves through their bodies, the expressions and gestures that the author can only describe in words. (2004, 3)

In other words, the true value of combining dramatic play with literacy learning is in the physical experience of the story as the children play inside the events. The words on the page come fully alive as the children embody the story.

Dramatic play works best when the teacher finds a place in the story that is worth further exploration. Determining this place is often driven by a big question or big idea that will lead into a lived-through experience. Big ideas focus on broader concepts that usually emerge from children's investigations. They are framed in big questions that give children lots of room to explore on many different levels. Although big ideas may emerge from a child's curiosity, they will be framed by your research and the children's as you collaborate on the dramatic story's construction. The question "Why did they have to leave everything behind?" regarding an immigrant experience can lead to a big story that children explore together from many points of view.

The dramatic play that is born out of the initial question might be brief or might go on for several days depending on the momentum and interest of the children. There may, for example, be a place in the story where the family gathers. The teacher might stop the story at that point to invite the class to become the family while she listens for the children's own conversation and interpretation of the event. This brief play experience would be designed to move the children into the real-life context of the story and to give the teacher insights into the children's comprehension and use of language.

Experiencing perspectives: An illustration

One effective way of using dramatic play with story is where the conflict or tension is building. At this point it is ideal for children to live inside the conflict from at least two perspectives in order to explore attitudes and points of view. For *Feathers and Fools* by Mem Fox, for example, the children could explore being peacocks and then swans. They could act as the birds in the story act and gossip about one another, speculating on what the others are doing, taking turns strutting like peacocks and then being graceful like swans. It is valuable for them to experience both sides of such a story, lifting the words off the page and giving the story a physical presence. Dramatic play works between the lines, in this case, to help the children understand some of the attitudes and language choices that are conveyed, but may not be expressed directly by the author. In *Feathers and Fools*, Mem Fox writes: "There followed anxious mutterings and a making of plans." What might that look like and sound like if the children were being the peacocks?

Staying inside the Story

"One of the problems of 'acting out' a known story is that the children already know how it ends. And we thereby not only miss out on valuable learning opportunities, but can also lose the dramatic tension of not knowing what will happen next . . . If we use a known story as a starting point, we should think how we can explore it, open it up, keep some dramatic tension alive."

— Woolland (1993, 18)

Since the focus on dramatic play is to invite children to live through an experience, to "test the waters," and to deepen their understanding, working with story requires finding places in the story that might be fun, difficult, or tense, or may simply need to be clarified through further dramatic investigation.

In *Where the Wild Things Are* by Maurice Sendak, the experience of Max being sent to bed without any supper is simply one line: ". . . so he was sent to bed without eating anything." The typical teacher question might be to stop the story and ask the children if they have ever been sent to bed without any supper and to describe what it might be like. In dramatic play, however, the teacher invites the children to curl up in their imaginary beds as Max; she then circulates among them, tapping each child (see Tapping In, on page 45) and asking, *"Max, how are you feeling?"* She might add that she can hear the child's tummy rumbling, note that the child is tossing and turning, or ask what food the child did not get to eat at supper.

If the teacher takes on a character herself, her interactions with the children will be different. Taking on a role can help the children empathize with their character, especially if the teacher is working within a text. The teacher in role can provide an opportunity for the children to more fully understand the situation that the character they are playing is experiencing. For instance, if in role as a stern parent, she could direct the children as Max to settle down and get to sleep. No doubt, there would be lots of giggles, but the children might also gain a sense of how Max felt.

There is a subtle difference between asking a question when the children are outside the story and asking the question when they are inside the story. When children are asked a question as story outsiders, they might be able to reflect on their own experiences or provide a detached opinion; however, asking them to answer from inside the story invites children to stay inside the story and feel what is going on. An inside-the-story question might be: *"Captain Tarik, the seas are rough and your crew is exhausted. Is it safe to set anchor?"* An outside-the-story question would halt the flow: *"Tarik, can you tell us how the captain might make a decision in rough seas?"* As the wise child quoted at the beginning of this chapter states, ". . . it is like walking in the pages of the book." Expanding the story through dramatic play investigation gets the words off the page for the early reader and provides the child with ways to respond and interpret through the familiar mode of play.

First of all, though, an appropriate story needs to be chosen.

Choosing a Story

When you choose a story, you will need to think about which parts of the story are most worthy of further exploration and what kind of dramatic play the story invites. Here are some questions to consider:

- Is there a big idea or a big question that the children can play in?
- Is there a conflict or tension worth living through?
- Are groups of people, animals, or even things struggling in a particular situation?
- Does the story have a flip side that is worth investigating? (For example, in a story about loss of habitat, what is the lumber company's perspective?)

- Is there a potential backstory that might deepen an understanding of the tension?
- Is there a situation in the story that would be clarified through dramatic play?
- Are there gaps that are important to fill in order to develop deeper understanding?
- Is part of the story difficult to comprehend and so could be understood better through dramatic play?

Always regard the play experience as an opportunity to learn more about the children and their sense of what is going on and how they perceive the story. Whether you stop the story as you are reading it to explore an idea or return to it after it has been read to explore the idea does not really matter. Exploring an idea before it is read, however, provides a heightened motivation and excitement to read the story independently once part of it has been lived in dramatically.

Going Deeper: Experiencing Cinderella's Plight

The Grade 1 students were studying fairy tales. They had a number of books that told the story of Cinderella in a few different ways, but the children were not connecting with Cinderella's plight as a servant. Although lots of princess play occurred during play time, it seemed important to take them deeper into the story: to understand more of what it was like to be mistreated and unloved and then be transformed and liberated.

Cinderella the Servant

The dramatist gathered the students on the carpet and asked them to identify some of the jobs that Cinderella had to do in the house of her stepmother. They made a substantial list. Then the dramatist asked if they would like to practice being Cinderella doing these jobs. Their response was enthusiastic except that a few of the boys objected to being a girl — being Cinder-fella, however, appealed to them. The children were prompted to find a place in the classroom where they, as Cinderella (or Cinder-fella), would be working. They scattered and began scrubbing, sweeping, washing, sewing, hammering, and generally having a great deal of fun.

Teacher in role as stepmother

The students then came back to the carpet to discuss their various jobs, and the dramatist asked if she could play the role of the stepmother (see Chapter 7 on teacher in role). They cautiously agreed. To test how stern she could be in this role, the dramatist got several children to volunteer as Cinderella while she as stepmother escalated her demands. Each step of the way the dramatist asked the children if her actions were cruel enough for her character.

After a brief discussion the children all agreed to return to their places and begin work again, more seriously this time as the stepmother circulated and aggressively reprimanded and criticized them. *"Keep your head down." "That's not good enough." "Stop talking." "Do that again." "Work harder." "There will be no break today."* As she moved through the classroom, she watched carefully to monitor the children's response, knowing the individuals who would require a more gentle approach.

"In role you can be far more harsh both verbally and nonverbally than you dare be as teacher," Betty Jane Wagner noted in *Educational Drama and Language Arts*, "thereby heightening the drama and feeding the class cues in a way that is not possible as a teacher" (1998, 132). The children giggled as the stepmother circulated among them, but they also remained focused on their tasks, continuing to wash, scrub, hammer, and dust.

Later, back on the carpet, the Grade 1 students again discussed how it felt to be subject to the whims of the stepmother. The children were now deeply into their roles as Cinderella, understanding how she must have felt and how she must have longed for an escape.

Tapping in to dreams

At this point the children were invited to pretend that they were in their room at night, talking to themselves about their hopes for a better life. Several of the children immediately curled up on the carpet, and others followed. Slowly, the dramatist moved among them, tapping each one on the shoulder and asking, *"Cinderella, what do you dream about?"* Most of them stayed within the context of the story: "I am dreaming of some nice clothes." "I am dreaming of not having to work so hard." Some of the boys, however, shared dreams of being hockey stars. Every response was affirmed.

After another brief discussion on this part of their experience, the students as Cinderella (or Cinder-fella) returned to their chores, and this time, the dramatist in role as Fairy Godmother appeared with a makeshift wand. She called all the Cinderellas and Cinder-fellas to meet her in the "scullery." The children did not know what a scullery was, but they dutifully returned to the carpet to meet with the Fairy Godmother. They eagerly told her their own stories of hardship and drudgery and shared their desire to escape to the ball. Some of the children even pretended to cry. Others simply made a statement. Still others were silent.

Transforming into guests for the ball

The next step was a transformation from rags to gown (for the boys, rags to tuxedo). The children discussed what they would wear and what the process of change might look like. Together, they tried out several variations. To the slow beat of a drum, they began to mime their transformation. They practiced this several times, each time adding more detail, perhaps putting on a tiara, special gloves, a cummerbund, or a bow tie. Back they went to their jobs and then to the teacher's slow beating of the drum, each child transformed into someone ready to be presented at the prince's fancy dress ball. The Fairy Godmother with her wand moved among them.

As you can see, the story took on a deeper significance for the children. By living through the experience and willingly suspending disbelief, the children felt a deeper connection to the character's plight. They came closer to understanding that the story goes beyond a young woman wanting to go to a ball.

Ways to Expand Understanding

"A 21st-century view of comprehension places emphasis on deep understanding, not on the number of books read or words written. Comprehension is not about memorizing facts and being literal. Across disciplines understanding must be actively created."

— Cornett (2001, 13)

Dramatic play builds on comprehension that is actively created in partnership with children. Dramatic play invites students to respond and reflect in a specific role, put on different characters with different perspectives, and explore various interpretations of a story, all in support of helping students expand their understanding of a story or theme.

Tap in during quiet moments

As indicated in the Cinderella example, Tapping In is an excellent way for children to respond reflectively in role. As in many dramatic play experiences, Tapping In may require practice for the children to recognize that their reflections and points of view are valued. It also demonstrates that there are many ways to interpret a single event. The strategy is most effective when used during story moments that require a pause: for example, the group is about to leave, is resting, is hiding out, or feels frightened. As an opportunity for reflection, Tapping In provides children with time to identify their own emotional responses. It serves to slow the children down and helps gives the story a depth of feeling sometimes overlooked when the child is grappling with words on a page.

Allow the children to play several roles

In theatre, roles are designated. When we re-enact a story or develop a script, we may find ourselves tempted to hand out roles to children. In dramatic play, however, we want as many children as possible to experience as much as possible. Perhaps you noticed that when the children explored *Where the Wild Things Are*, all of them were Max. If we pursued this play experience further, all of the children would be the Wild Things, too. Inviting children to play a variety of roles takes the pressure off individuals and exposes many variables in terms of the interpretation of events. It will facilitate a deeper comprehension of the story or theme.

Explore one story from a range of different perspectives

This kind of exploration takes the story beyond the book and moves it into other dimensions that might be considered. It thereby enriches children's imaginations and expands the original story. When children explore a story from the perspectives of different characters or viewpoints, they are encouraged to see and understand the story in different ways, perhaps to empathize with the villain or consider an issue from another's point of view. Their exploration can yield many different interpretations of the same story. Children playing in "The Pied Piper," for example, could dramatically interpret the story from the varying perspectives of the rats, the overwhelmed cats, and the Mayor and the Town Council, who have to decide whether or not to believe the Piper; the students could even approach the story as a community of pied pipers telling tales and sharing techniques for ridding communities of rats.

Exploring the dimensions of a story involves your own wondering and wandering with the children in conversation, encouraging their curiosity, and inviting them to consider what to try in dramatic play. The children may see the main character in the story as one dimensional and not consider the emotional qualities of the character's experience. If so, they could be given an opportunity to be the character in a similar situation through Tapping In and then write in role to express some of the emotions they imagine the character felt.

Children may be caught up in the action of the story and so need help in considering consequences from another's point of view. Consider "The Three Billy Goats Gruff." The alternative to taking turns "trip, trapping" over the bridge might be for the children to go in role as trolls. Perhaps they are wondering about their friend under the bridge. What would the trolls be thinking and discussing?

For the arts curriculum document, see http://www.edu.gov.on.ca/eng/curriculum/elementary/arts18b09curr.pdf.

Might there be negotiations with the billy goats? The teacher, in this case, could play a troll and lead the discussion through questions that draw the children into the story.

Developing the ability to see and understand a range of perspectives is valuable. In the words of the *Ontario Arts Curriculum, Grades 1 to 8: The Arts, 2009*: "As students 'live through' experiences of others in imagined situations, they learn to understand a variety of points of view and motives and to empathize with others. This exploration of the 'as if' in roles and worlds will help students deepen their understanding of humanity and issues of equity and social justice." Dramatic play promotes empathy and a sense of social justice.

Your Role within a Story

Your role in dramatic play within a story is significant. As both a listener and an observer, you will need to move slowly step by step with the children, giving them time to be in the story but also coming out of the story to discuss and reflect on the experience. Part of your role is to hear the children's perspective, to wonder with them, to explore suggestions with them, and to note the many variations in interpreting the story.

As dramatist, you will constantly be on the lookout for opportunities to extend the dramatic story. Recognizing opportunities is perhaps the most difficult task. You may feel uncertain about doing this because it is based on listening to the children, not following the story verbatim. The dramatist listens for suggestions from children that would deepen their understanding or move the story into an interesting place. For example, consider the children who curled up and went to sleep as Max. Doing that significantly deepened their comprehension of the story. The dramatist supported their response by creating a bedtime atmosphere. She turned out the lights and moved quietly among the children, encouraging them to describe their dreams.

Your role as dramatist also involves recognizing and valuing how children play. You may have to self-monitor many times to stop yourself from interrupting the children's play. For example, curling up under a desk or standing on a chair may be absolutely necessary for a child to explore a role. You may see this behavior as potential danger, but taking the risk safely along with the child in such situations is part of recognizing how children play.

A Selection of Classic Stories for Dramatic Play

The Highway Rat by Julia Donaldson, illustrated by Axel Scheffler
    Advice: Stop reading aloud just before the rat meets the duck.
    Children can play as animals having things stolen, telling their stories.
    Issue: What should be done about the Highway Rat?
The Mitten by Jan Brett
    Advice: Play inside sections of the story.
    Children decide which animals to be and plan the actions of the story.
    Issue: What should they tell Baba, the boy's grandmother?

Feathers and Fools by Mem Fox, illustrated by Nicholas Wilton

> *Advice:* Read only the first few pages.
>
> Children can pretend to be the peacocks and then the swans. Use the Tapping In and working with rumors strategies.
>
> *Issue:* How can the swans and peacocks resolve their differences?

The Stranger by Chris Van Allsberg

> *Advice:* Read up to the curious turning of the leaves.
>
> The town meets to discuss the stranger and the strange things happening on Farmer Bailey's farm.
>
> *Issue:* What is going on with Farmer Bailey and his land?

Where the Wild Things Are by Maurice Sendak

> *Advice:* Break up the story between Max and the Wild Things.
>
> Let the children first be Max and then later the Wild Things discussing their "Rumpus."
>
> *Issue:* What does Max have to say about meeting the Wild Things? What do the Wild Things think about Max? How do they plan the Rumpus?

The Great Kapok Tree by Lynne Cherry

> *Advice:* Stop reading aloud when the man falls asleep.
>
> Have the animals meet to discuss what to do about the man with the axe.
>
> *Issue:* What can the animals do to protect their environment?

The Crane Girl by Veronika Martenova Charles

> *Advice:* Stop reading aloud when the cranes find Yoshiko.
>
> Eventually, Yoshiko dances with the cranes, but much has to be resolved first.
>
> *Issue:* What should the cranes do with Yoshiko?
> (Have them gather to discuss the matter.)

Improvising a Story

Into Others' Shoes

"Dramatic improvisation is concerned with what we discover for ourselves and the group when we place ourselves in a human situation containing some element of desperation. Very simply it means putting ourselves into other people's shoes and, by using personal experience to help you understand their point of view, you may discover more than you knew when you started."

— Dorothy Heathcote, in Johnson and O'Neill (1984, 44)

Stories may emerge quite naturally from the children, or you may want to develop an improvised story that can augment an investigation. Improvising a story is an exciting way to work, but it is also risky in that it is a mystery in terms of how it will evolve. The power of the improvised story, however, is that it is almost completely developed by the children and provides ample writing opportunities during and at the end of the dramatic play experience.

An improvised story may come from the children who are interested in exploring something quite apart from what they are studying. If you ask them what they would like to make a story about, you will probably hear many references to TV and video games along with travels to the moon and who knows what! This discussion is usually animated, and you will need to decide which suggestions will provide the best dramatic play situation. Here are some questions to consider:

- Can all the children participate? Remember that, in dramatic play everyone can be everything all the time. Roles do not need to be designated, although roles might emerge as the story progresses.
- Can this situation be a complex one rather than a simple one? Consider whether there is an issue, problem, tension, or big idea worth exploring.
- Do you think you have enough time to complete the story within the frame you have committed? Consider how much class time you can set aside to further the story's exploration.

- Are appropriate resources available? You may need to search for resources that will augment the story so that the children's play becomes richer and fuller.
- What will you need to begin? It may be important to begin dramatic play with an object that intrigues, a different space, or an atmosphere (perhaps set by lights turned off, music, or sound).

The beginning as hook

In Chapter 3, we considered the importance of practice to establish authenticity, develop skills, and try out a number of approaches even before dramatic play begins. Because developing an improvised story is play, not scripted performance, the beginning point is crucial for establishing the story. Initiating a beginning that will hold the imagination of the children is also an opportunity to assess where the children are, which helps you plan the next phase. The beginning will provide the hook or lure that creates the excitement and commitment to pursue ideas further. It should give the children a good reason to continue. Remember, however, not to make the highest action the starting point but rather, prepare the children to take action through stillness, observation, and practice.

Prompting Improvisation: Strategies

There are a variety of creative and concrete ways to launch an improvised story.

Plant a letter. An interesting way to begin an improvised story is with a letter that you have composed. Suppose the children agree that their story should be about a space mission. Imagine their surprise when one child finds an official-looking envelope on his desk addressed to the class the next day. After perhaps ignoring it for a while, the children beg you to open the envelope. You discover it is a letter from the Space Centre commissioning them to prepare for the next voyage to Mars.

The letter is the cause of much excitement. Knowing your class, you can probably sense the momentum the letter will create for planning and research as the students discuss their roles and what they need for the expedition. They may even decide they need to build a space ship, and they will certainly need to find out about food, space suits, communication, planet atmosphere, and much, much more. In the meantime, you will be preparing resources: identifying appropriate websites, taking out books from the library, and finding pictures and models to set up for the next day's exploration.

Fill in with research. Improvised stories often require an expansion of detail. The question to ask yourself is whether or not more detailed information will support and further the story. Filling in is necessary when you and the children recognize that more information is, indeed, required before the story can continue. You may, for example, stop the story because you realize that the children have little understanding of who other than a princess might live in a castle. This is an ideal time to investigate further. The motivation for research gains a whole new momentum when children have a need to find out more. The librarian and the Internet become central to the filling-in period.

Begin with a setting. Establishing the setting will support the improvised story. Quickly changing the configuration of desks, chairs, and tables may be necessary. You may want to invite the children to find individual spaces that further suggest who they are in the story. You could also have them practice coming into a space in order to gain a sense of who the characters are and where their story will begin.

Base the improvised story on an object. Improvised stories can often be prompted by such objects as a recruiting poster on the door, a pirate chest with a map, and a series of gigantic dinosaur footprints leading to the window. Piquing children's curiosity and sense of wonder cannot be underestimated in the play experience. If the object fascinates the children and creates speculation, you can be assured that a dramatic story is about to begin.

As the children discuss their ideas and theories with regard to the object, you will need to listen carefully for the one contribution that can begin the dramatic play. The dramatic story might simply be the children taking action as advocates in an imaginary situation. Perhaps the children think that the dinosaur footprints were made by a lost dinosaur. They may want to go into role as dinosaurs and help the lost dinosaur find his way back home. This story development may lead to a final note left by the dinosaur that was lost or a scene with the teacher in role as the dinosaur (see Chapter 7). The experience can help the class explore what it is like to have helping friends.

Beginning with an object: Pirates in search of treasure

The Treasure Map   The Grade 4 students were exploring the topic of pirates. They already had seen movies and read stories about pirate life. They had also developed backstories about how they became pirates (see the writing-in-role excerpt on page 48). However, they lacked understanding of the organization and planning required to follow a map and look for clues in order to discover treasure. The teacher wanted the children to play together as pirates and hunt for treasure. She was eager to encourage them to play.

The class's improvised story began with a small chest, which had been set on a child's desk. There was a map inside it. Instantly, the children were excited and curious. Of course, they wanted to hunt for the treasure as individuals. The tension mounted as an argument broke out about who got to hold the treasure chest!

The dramatist, playing the role of pirate captain, gathered them on the carpet and in role explained to them that they needed to get organized since their pirates' motto was "All for one and one for all." After chanting their motto several times, the children settled in to examining the treasure map. They were to work as a team to follow the clues together, but before they could do that, they needed to learn how to use the compass in order to find directions accurately. Meanwhile, the teacher and dramatist had planted riddles throughout the school and playground. Each riddle, rolled up and tied with string, led to the next. A typical one was "Westward roam to number four, look up high and on the floor." This riddle led students, using their compasses, down the west hallway to Room 4, where another clue was planted under a table outside the door. At the end of the pirates' hunt were two treasure chests in the sand box at the far corner of the playground. These chests were loaded with enough "jewels" for each of the children.

How Dramatic Play Unfolds: Expanding the Story of Icarus

The multi-age class of students in Grades 1, 2, and 3 were studying Greek mythology, using a range of resources. The story of Icarus was of great interest, but the teacher wondered if expanding the part of the story in which Icarus is captive in the tower might give the students a better understanding of confinement and of Icarus' ultimate need to escape.

Icarus in captivity

Imprisoned in the Tower

The dramatist read a version of the story up to the time Icarus was put into captivity. She then asked the children for their ideas about the tower and what it might be like to spend months and years in a tower with only one window. She prompted them to describe the space. The children responded with words such as *cold*, *damp*, and *lonely*.

The dramatist then asked them to come together in a tight cluster, outlining on the carpet the tower's circumference. One child suggested that the space should be dark so the dramatist turned out the lights. As the class sat silently, she used Tapping In, asking each child what he or she missed from life in the outside world. Their responses indicated that they were fully into the story and sensing what it would have been like to be held in a tower or at least in a dark, restricted place.

Icarus striving to escape

Later on the dramatist wanted the children to better understand how difficult it must have been for Icarus to capture birds and pluck their feathers in order to make wings. A chair was set up with a large feather under it. She told the children that she would be a bird on the windowsill of the tower and that they were to sneak up and grab the feather without the bird hearing or seeing them and flying away. They enjoyed the game and also realized that the plucking was no simple task for Icarus. For them the story had been deepened and their imaginations expanded beyond the words on the page.

The students later made a study of bird wings, which involved them in measuring, mathematics, predicting, and problem solving. When they had finished making wings, they went to the gym to fly out of the tower, which was represented by a bench. Since the children seemed to be fully in the story, there was little need to change anything in the gym. Some escapees chose to fly too close to the imaginary sun and die a tragic death, while others flew successfully to Crete!

SUMMARY
- Look and listen for story possibilities in which children can actively participate.
- Weigh whether the story is worthy of further exploration.
- Begin where the conflict or tension is building, not with the highest action, at least without preparing the children first.
- Choose a starting point that will spark the students' interest.
- Listen for opportunities suggested by the children.
- Approach a story's conflict from different points of view, inviting children to examine various interpretations and roles.
- Take a risk along with the children.
- Use specially prepared letters and strategically chosen objects to stimulate improvisation.
- Practice, and plan next steps.

---

6 Playing inside Curriculum

> "Emergent curriculum is sensible but not predictable. It requires of its practitioners trust in the power of play — trust in spontaneous choice making among many possibilities. Good programs for young children encourage children to become competent players."
> — Elizabeth Jones and John Nimma, *Emergent Curriculum* (p. 1)

Motivating children's interest in the usual curriculum inquiry can sometimes be challenging; dramatic play, however, changes the nature of curriculum investigation with an invitation to play inside the events and big ideas. When children are given opportunities to explore through play, there is a definite shift in their interest and motivation. Suddenly, what perhaps seemed disconnected and uninteresting becomes personal and up close. A momentum is created, driving the children's need to find out more. With their curiosity heightened, research becomes a natural next step.

In curriculum, the dramatic play experience can move quickly from the facts to the emotional tensions embedded in the situation. When children recognize that there are emotional tensions, they are likely to become involved in a meaningful understanding of the curriculum event you are pursuing. What appears at first to be a simple historical fact may have emerged from an emotionally charged debate. For example, the choice of the present red-and-white Canadian flag grew out of a heated debate between veterans, who preferred the original flag, and Prime Minister Lester B. Pearson, who preferred the design of a new flag. We often forget the emotional aspects buried in stories in science (e.g., the impact of a dwindling resource) and in social studies: these stories can involve difficult decisions, challenging events, disputes, disagreements, and multiple points of view. Dramatic play can highlight these and heighten student engagement.

Establishing a Framework for Investigation

As in most dramatic play experiences, playing inside curriculum begins with story. Social Studies, Science, and Language Arts are full of rich stories that lend themselves to a lived-through experience. As reflected in Chapter 5, look for stories in curriculum that have tension or that point to complex issues that can involve the children in living through experiences. Look for places in the story in which children can build a background together, perhaps as a family, as insects, as a flock, as a political party, as workers. Are there certain events that are worth playing together in, for example, travelling, protesting, planning, plotting, taking part in rituals and ceremonies, or constructing?

Once you have found a curriculum-based story that you believe will capture the children's imagination, you will need to construct a framework that outlines the key areas you intend to investigate with them. These are the elements of the story that are worthy of further attention: that will deepen the children's understanding of the experience they are about to live through. Remember that the framework is not a script but rather an outline that is open enough to enable the children to shape the response within the event.

The framework that you plan can also be a step-by-step walk through the story in concert with children suggesting or filling in the events that they believe to be important steps along the way. Essentially, this "walk" is the practice period as the children plan out the actions that will take place. This kind of lived-in experience works best with subjects in which the children already have some knowledge but may not have a clear understanding of all the details, for example, of how a plant grows or how a particular occupation is carried out. In the co-constructed approach, the teacher solicits possibilities from the children that begin the play process. For each step, the teacher invites the children to shape the story.

Questions on which to base a framework

Developing a dramatic play framework begins with five essential questions:
1. Which event carries the most significance and the most opportunities for living through an experience?
2. Does the lived experience provide lots of room for children to investigate further in multiple ways?
3. What aspects of the story will "hook" the children's curiosity?
4. What parts of the story can be problematized to create dramatic tension?
5. What filling in of details or research will be necessary once the story has begun?

Addressing these questions provides a way to begin developing a dramatic play framework. But, first of all, your imagination is required to uncover the potential curriculum story, looking for that one sentence or idea that sparks your imagination or the one event that carries significant tensions.

Issues to Explore: Possible Curriculum-Related Examples

- A habitat is threatened.
- A group in the past must leave their homeland.
- Well water is contaminated.
- A government faces a dilemma before a vote.
- A woodlot must make way for a housing development.
- A family confronts a new way of life.
- Insects worry about the use of toxic chemicals.
- Trees discuss how they are not being used sustainably.
- One group is threatened by either physical violence or dangerous ideas from another group.

Each of these big ideas holds a story that a group of children could live through.

Identifying the Tension: Two Examples

1. In an investigation of an early civilization, you discover this paragraph: "Priests owned slaves who worked for them in the temples, and wealthy families owned slaves who worked for their family. Slaves worked to pay off debts. People became slaves if their parents or husbands sent them, or they could be born into slavery. They could also buy their way to freedom."
Retrieved from http://meso-potamiadiv1.wikispaces.com/The+Class+System+and+Education+in+Mesopotamia
You identify the following provocation to explore: Could a slave ever be free?

2. The needs of living things is a topic in Science. A tension is that a flower garden is wilting away. What might the flowers say in a discussion of how they can grow strong?

Choosing how to use dramatic play

Whether or not the children have information about the area of study depends on how you want to use dramatic play. If it is to initiate the story, bring forward questions, and spur on an inquiry, then little information is required. If you want students to make use of research they have done already, however, then the initial event will be a building block for the story to develop further and for the children to feel the human elements within the story as they deliberate in role. Remember that dramatic play "muddies the waters," or treats a situation as a problem to be solved, so the initial gathering needs to challenge the group and put them into a predicament not easily resolved. By establishing the point of tension you are inviting the children to not only discuss possible solutions but to establish their identities within the story. Your role in the beginning scenario is to act as one of the group who keeps the dialogue going. Once the group has gathered, you can present the *who*, *what*, *where*, and *why* of the issue in your initial statement and then wonder, question, and explore along with the children.

Getting into the Curriculum Story: Approaches

As in other kinds of stories, dramatic play experiences based on the curriculum rely on appropriately defining the play space, practicing roles in context, and preparing the children to enter the space as believable characters.

Define the play space

Inviting the class to organize the play space so it feels like the environment of the event they are about to embark on is important (see Chapter 4). Creating an appropriate space provides a transition from classroom setting to the world of dramatic play. It also gives children an opportunity to become involved at the very beginning.

Creation of the setting in the play space can owe much to the imagination. The carpet can become everything from a secret hiding place to a pond to a clearing in a forest. Your role here is to ask for suggestions. *"Where might this story take place? Do we need to arrange anything to help us believe we are really there?"* No doubt, there will be numerous suggestions, and it will be up to you and the children to decide. Simply rearranging the desks or tables, for example, can suggest a more formal gathering for a board meeting or a government setting.

Sometimes, the lights might need to be dimmed or turned off — especially if the event takes place in secret or occurs outside at night.

Objects representing a particular time period or a specific predicament can serve as symbols and reference points throughout the story and help focus the group as they proceed. A trunk, a photo, a map, a blanket — almost anything can symbolize a historical period. For example, a trunk might represent an immigrant family coming to a new land; a photo, a working farm at harvest time; an old map vague in details, an explorer's starting point; and a blanket, a fiercely cold pioneer winter.

Carefully chosen and placed objects can also provide the beginning of the story. The teacher might say: *"I found this poster outside the post office. It says we have to leave. I don't know about you, but I am heartbroken that it has come to this."* The students could then go on to investigate the group that had been targeted to leave.

Get into character and context

It is always important to take the time to practice being in character. For children, taking on a role often requires a step-by-step layering of who they are as they practice becoming the character. This process might be as simple as transforming into an individual animal from the feet to the top of the head or as complex as establishing a family grouping in a historical setting. Backing up from the beginning of the story and laying in the groundwork necessary for children to build their identity is crucial.

In a community or a historical setting, it may be necessary for the students to establish family groupings and name who they are. Looking at pictures of family groupings, such as that below, will help build this sense of who they are, as will making sketches of relevant groupings and their homes or environment.

Images, such as this photo of an immigrant family arriving at Ellis Island, New York, can be found at Google Images. Archives Canada (www.archivescanada.ca) may also be worth investigating. A wealth of images is available online.

There are a variety of ways to deepen this initial commitment through filling in details about the participants. This is where writing in role by students in older grades can help establish an identity. Writing can be continued throughout the drama as the students make journal entries about their experiences within the story.

Call a meeting with everyone in role

The initial dramatic play experience often begins with a group meeting in which the children gather as the people or animals confronting a difficult question. Through the meeting everyone is brought together to take the first steps of being in the story, and who the children are, where they are, and what they are about to confront are clarified.

Once the meeting place is established, the next step is for the children to get into role in order to come to the meeting in such a way that they are believable. Whether they are animals or humans, they will need to prepare or practice their roles as an important first step to living inside the story. As the animals slither, hop, and fly, or perhaps as the people tiptoe to a secret meeting to plan an escape or discuss an offer, you will need to assess whether the children are in or still out of the story. In other words, can you see that they are taking on their characters and are believable? They may need to practice their arrival several times before their focus seems obvious. Only then can the story begin.

Finding the Story in Social Studies

Story in curriculum can be inspired in a variety of ways. For example, you might encounter a sentence in reading through the curriculum that makes you wonder about the backstory or the events leading up to what the statement conveys. Or a story or picture book that you read to your students might reveal their interest in and desire to know more about a situation. Here are a few titles that may prompt their interest, with suggested grade levels:

- *Jeremiah Learns to Read* by Jo Ellen Bogart, illustrated by Laura Fernandez, Rick Jacobson, and Fernandez R. Jacobson (Grades 3 and 4)
- *Across the Alley* by Richard Michelson, illustrated by E. B. Lewis (Grade 3)
- *Night Shift* by Jessie Hartland (Grades 2 and 3)
- *A Promise Is a Promise* by Robert Munsch and Michael Kusugak, illustrated by Vladyana Krykorka (Grades 1 and 2)
- *Angel Child, Dragon Child* by Michele Maria Surat, illustrated by Vo Dinh Mai (Grade 1)
- *As Long as the River Flows* by Larry Loyie with Constance Brissenden as contributor, illustrated by Heather D. Holmlund (Grade 4)

Many social studies curricula stress the need for children to be able to explain their decisions and to be aware of more than one point of view — dramatic play lends itself to playing several perspectives. A topic such as the importance of government and citizenship may bring to mind the backstory of how decisions are made on behalf of others. The class in role as the local government may meet to discuss the development of a suburb, factory, or business on a vacant lot in a park or near the school. Children first playing governing officials can flip to being citizens with a petition for the governing body to consider. The power of dramatic play is that it affords an opportunity to play a number of sides followed by a rich discussion based on the children's emotional responses as well as their cognitive and imaginative investment in the story.

An exciting lived-through possibility might arise through your own research of a topic. Something captures your imagination and you can envision how the children in your class might respond. Perhaps a study of an ancient civilization reveals a possibility for the students to live through a certain ritual or ceremony, and you can readily see the beginning point and how the events might be organized in a framework for the children.

Sometimes, a story emerges because a child asks a question that is worth pursuing, such as "Why did they have to leave their homes?" Asking the children if they would like to explore this further through play will inevitably lead to the shaping of a framework that will take the students through the significant events that led up to people leaving.

There is no question that the social studies curriculum is full of stories that you can find and tap into to provide your students with rich experiences. The advantage of playing in a historical story is that children have the opportunity to live out its human dimensions, something that propels them beyond the historical events and facts. Dramatic play affords them time to explore history as the people who lived it, giving them a better sense of the fear, the uncertainty, the tensions, and the confusion. It presents a different picture of history than what students might first have: one that is complex rather than a simple linear outline of individuals and events.

A step-by-step co-constructed experience in dramatic play

Firefighting The social studies curriculum may require that students examine the roles and responsibilities of people in a local community. The children or the teacher may decide to look more closely at the role of firefighters, for example. In the children's minds, the firefighter simply puts out a fire and when they re-enact this, their play is full of running, wailing like a siren, and making rushing sounds for the water in the hose.

A Kindergarten class had been studying the unit People Who Help in the Community. A firefighter had visited the classroom, and the children were excited by trying on his helmet and his very large and heavy jacket. Noting their enthusiasm the classroom teacher invited the dramatist to play out a fire-fighting scenario with the children.

The following is a step-by-step outline of the questions the dramatist used for the whole class to become firefighters.

Step 1 — *Where might the fire hall be in the classroom?* Once location was established, other objects (a telephone, some pillows) were added to make the space into the fire hall. Letting the children decide is important.

Step 2 — *Where will the fire be in the room?* Here, the teachers recommended that the fire be as far away from the fire hall as possible to facilitate travel — children sometimes require an adult to make a decision. It was decided that a house would burn.

Step 3 — *What should we build the house of?* The Kindergarten students knew instantly how to build a house from the blocks in the room. They were very organized. Several children added stuffed animals to the house for the firefighters to rescue. Children understand the basic needs of play: how to build a house, what props are necessary, and what items can symbolize what.

Step 4 — *Let's establish our route to the house . . .* Because this activity could be quite chaotic, the dramatist led the children through the classroom in a follow-the-leader style. They later followed the route on their own.

Step 5 — Having a rough draft of the main play spaces, the children met back at the fire hall. The dramatist asked: "*What do firefighters do in the fire hall?*" The children had lots of ideas. Some played, some curled up for a nap, and others read storybooks. You, too, will want to encourage children to give multiple responses.

Step 6 — *How do the firefighters know that there is a fire?* The children responded with many suggestions, offering sounds and signals. They agreed on one cue: a shrill "woo, woo" with a few personal variations! Consensus may or may not always be possible.

Step 7 — *What do the firefighters do when they hear the alarm?* Because the visiting firefighter had discussed this with them, the students were aware of boots, pants, coat, and helmet. They mimed putting these on several times as practice. These kinds of ritual actions are important in establishing a willing suspension of disbelief.

Step 8 — *How do we get to the fire?* Here again, the dramatist helped the children get organized as a fire truck and take turns being the driver. The truck was a simple line-up affair with one person at the front steering — the steering was the most attractive. The students found this a great deal of fun and practiced several times.

Step 9 — *Now that we are at the burning house, what do we do? How long is the hose? Who will be first to rescue the people?* Addressing these questions required a bit of organization as the children wanted to take turns holding the imaginary hose and rescuing the stuffed animals (see the text box "Mimed versus Symbolic Props" below). This activity was practiced many times with lots of side-coaching, this time from the children.

Once the step-by-step practice was completed, the whole story of the firefighters was re-enacted again without the questions. The Kindergarten students requested this "play" again and again!

Mimed versus Symbolic Props

It is intriguing to observe how children use props in their dramatic play. In the firefighters' story, the children felt no need of anything to represent a fire hose; they were content to mime it. They did, however, require blocks to build the house and stuffed animals to rescue. It appears that mimed props in dramatic play are those that are either not significant to the story's momentum or those that need to be manifested quickly (as in the fire hose). Peeling a potato, riding a horse, washing dishes, and getting dressed are all part of the pretend vocabulary. Symbolic props, however, are a good stand-in for the real thing — a pencil can be a log; a block, a cell phone; a bench, a cliff; or a rolled-up piece of paper, a spyglass. The teacher's role is to ask the children what will suffice.

Framing Historical Stories

Because history has already been written, there is an outline of key events that you may wish to use as a framework for the story. These events are what the children will explore together, living through each segment, practicing, trying different points of view, interpreting, and reinterpreting if necessary.

Pausing is always an option in dramatic play but at this initial stage, building the story may be more important than stopping and starting again. Give the children ample time to absorb and speak about the issue, and assess whether enough information and roles are being established. Once satisfied, you will want to stop the story and invite the children to discuss what they know so far about the situation. You will especially want to hear their thoughts about who they are and what their circumstances are. No doubt, they will have many questions, and these will become the platform for further research; in turn, the research will provide them with a clearer picture of the problem before them when they enter the next stage.

Coloring-in the story picture

Filling in detail, or in-filling, deepens belief. Research, writing in role, drawing, mapping, and other activities clarify or "color in" the details of the picture. The effort to fill in may include writing in role to develop a backstory to clarify a character, mapping the present territory, reading a proclamation from the government, planning a protest, or sending a delegate to confront the people in power.

Filling in can be done in role, or it can be done out of role as a way of further researching a story. A proclamation might be first considered by the children out of role but be reconsidered within the story's context when they are in role. Writing in role can be used for reflection as the student continues to imagine himself in role, or the student can write in first-person singular and draw on fresh research pertaining to the role for details. Children playing in role might begin with an imaginary map but then research the map more specifically out of role in order to return to the map in their story with more specifics. This kind of detail seeking could be important if the dramatic play story is in conjunction with geography, for example.

A Framework Example: Leaving Home for a New Life

This extended outline is presented in rather general terms but could be adapted to apply to a particular group of immigrants, past or present.

Significant Event: A group of people are compelled to leave their homes. They are subject to limited choices, difficult and often desperate decisions, and strong feelings as they leave the familiar and travel into the unknown. They must settle in a new place.

Student-Generated Question: Why did people leave their homes and come here to settle?

Teacher Consideration of Possible Lived-Through Experiences: A community living in fear; secret meetings to plan leaving; discussion of how to earn money for passage; meeting with person in charge of transportation; issues of trust, fear of the unknown; leaving of the familiar for the unknown; looking at maps; discussing the future; wondering what to take; having trust in the process of leaving that they have chosen

Materials Used: A poster promising a better life; an official letter, either evicting or making a promise; the last bit of bread to share — any item that will symbolize the desperation of the group about to leave

Filling in the historical picture to build belief

- Organize students in family groupings.
- Use names from research for each family. Based on your own research, you might give the names to students in Grades 1 and 2, but let students in Grades 3 and 4 research their own on designated sites online or with the help of a librarian.
- Give each family group a section from a diary or a story told in first person. The diary can reflect the whole family group. Check online or in archives and the library for specific examples.
- Find appropriate pictures of landscape to give to each family group. Among possible groups are crofters leaving Scotland to settle in the Red River Valley,

When students are being grouped into families, focus mainly on adults. Babies create difficulties when children try to portray them!

United Empire Loyalists fleeing the United States, former slaves on the Underground Railroad, and Newfoundlanders moving to Alberta.

- Using the appropriate research as reference, have the students in their family groupings draw images of their house, their chosen mode of transportation, and significant items they might take with them.
- Prompt each group to create a tableau of the family unit — to pose for a picture.
- Introduce families to other families so that the students in their groupings get to know the other families. Doing this will also help build belief.
- Together, map the home village on a blank sheet of paper.

The initial meeting

In this section of the framework, the teacher will come in and out of role to practice, establish belief, consult with the children, pause for reflection and possible further in-filling, and build the momentum of the dramatic story. (See Chapter 7 for more information on teacher in role.)

- Organize the meeting space with the children. Discuss with them where and how a meeting should be held.
- While in role as a participating member of the group, call a meeting in secret to establish issue and tension.
- Let students practice entering in role. At this time, you are out of role.
- As teacher in role, invite rumors about the issue they need to confront.
- In role as part of the group, ask: *"What are you most fearful about? What are you most hopeful about?"*
- Prompt each family to tell a bit of its story. At this time, you could be in role or out of role. If students are not sincere, pause and discuss. Practice until they are. You are out of role.

Potent Paper
The symbol or object can be almost anything as long as the children believe it and as long as it is significant enough to hold the whole story. For example, a blank piece of paper can serve as a letter.

- Use a symbol or object to underline the difficulty that the group faces. Initially, you may be part of the group, taking the role of a group leader. You may switch roles later, if necessary, and work as teacher in role, coming out of role from time to time to get feedback and develop the next step.
- As a whole group, develop a plan for the departure. You may want to come in and out of role as the children consider their plan.

Preparing for and making the journey

The following suggestions recognize the likely need for more filling in of details. They can be considered with the children as the story of leaving home progresses.

- Invite the children to develop a list of goods necessary to sell in order to purchase passage or plan escape.
- Have the students research and draw images of items that might be taken with them.
- Use Tapping In with each student in role to find out what the prospective immigrant is thinking or dreaming about.
- Prompt the students to write in role as family members about what it means for them to leave.
- Carry out the agreed-upon plan, which will involve practice and be the direct result of the children's discussion. If high action is required, use tableaux or slow motion to establish belief.

- Have the students as immigrants make their journey, using the class space as earlier determined. Travel may be organized around the classroom, down the hall, or even outside depending on the story's circumstances.
- Let the students experience the arrival. You may want to set up a specific setting for the arrival — an immigration desk or land titles or employment office. If so, consider switching roles at this point to become an official or a welcoming host.

Experiencing History: Aboard *La Grande Hermine*

The Crew of *La Grande Hermine*, Part 2

Students in the Grades 4/5 class were studying explorers in Canadian history. The teacher had done this unit over and over again and was eager to make a change. "I really want the children to feel what it was like to prepare for a voyage to the New World," she said. With the dramatist, she selected several key points that would be worth living through with the children. What would engage the children in their own research and invite them to play inside the story of Jacques Cartier, an early explorer?

A poster was placed on the locked classroom door when the children arrived in the morning. They were immediately curious, and even while they stood at the door the dramatist sensed their rising energy. When the door opened, they burst into the classroom with an avalanche of questions. They met as usual on the carpet, and the teacher asked them if they would like to go on a pretend voyage with Jacques Cartier. The eagerness and excitement were palpable. "Would you like to meet the recruiter and see what she has to say?" They nodded enthusiastically. The teacher introduced the dramatist, who carried a very old book and swaggered into the circle.

"*So you would like to be part of Cartier's crew, would ya?*" she said in her gruffest voice. "*I don't know if you've got what it takes. You all look a little puny to me.*" (Laughter broke out.) "*It's no laughing matter being on board a ship and working your fingers to the bone for weeks,*" retorted the recruiter. "*What do you know about ships anyway?*"

Silence.

Finally, one boy raised a hand tentatively and replied, "Bow?"

"*Is that all you know? Surely, if you apply to be part of the crew, you will know more than that. I'm appalled! But Cartier said he's desperate so I suppose you'll have to do — I'll give you a week to get ready and then you can apply.*"

The recruiter strode away, leaving the children with a thousand questions.

Getting ready to be interviewed

Casting for Crew
A number of the positions students chose were not entirely authentic to the period, but were appropriate for dramatic play. Some historical licence can be taken in dramatic play in order to allow all children in the class to participate and to respect their desire to be part of the story. Women were not part of Cartier's original crew of 30, but it was important for the girls in the class to be part of this experience!

In the following week there was a flurry of research. Children chose their positions on the ship: gunner, carpenter, first mate, cabin girls, cook, entertainer, navigator, map reader, and regular deck hands. Their preparation for the recruiter's return was extensive and detailed. The teacher was amazed, and so was the dramatist when she returned as the recruiter.

Each child came forward for a job interview. The gunner applicant had made tiny replicas of sixteenth-century cannons out of Plasticine and proceeded to explain how a cannon was loaded and fired. The child hoping to be cabin girl brought in a silver tea service (compliments of her mom) to demonstrate how she would serve tea to Cartier as his cabin help. The prospective ship's cook had made biscuits (with her grandma) to serve everyone. The student wanting to be ship's entertainer brought her guitar and sang a lovely song to demonstrate her talents. All of the children presented their very best, and each one was hired and officially signed in as crew with a feather pen dipped in ink.

Creating Cartier's ship

Several days later the teacher, equally excited about the unfolding story, brought the children together to plan a ship in the middle of the classroom. They rearranged the tables and wrapped them in brown paper. Children inscribed *La Grande Hermine* on the ship's bow. They erected sails with metre sticks and large white paper, and the teacher brought in a white sheet that she strung up with ropes to look like the main sail.

La Grande Hermine, *as set up in the classroom*

On board — and off

The recruiter returned and the crew members boarded the ship across a gangplank. They pretended to haul sails, swab decks, cook, navigate, and so on until one of the boys fell overboard. This event could easily have been seen as a disruption, something that could have stopped the story, but within the context, it was legitimate. The focus on the rescue was exciting as the children hauled the boy back on deck. The ship's carpenter stepped in, announcing that as carpenter he was also the ship's surgeon. With great drama he sawed off the crew member's arm — much to the rescued sailor's delight. The one-armed sailor spent the rest of the day with his sleeve dangling loose!

The class went on to experiment with reading compasses on the playground, looking at ancient maps, learning the parts of a ship, writing accounts of their journey in first person, and drawing and describing their experiences on land. Their knowledge of ship life was so much richer because of their dramatic play experiences.

Finding the Story in Science

The science curriculum is full of stories, but you will need to look between the lines for those places that hint at a conflict, tension, or a problem. Some of the big themes in science are disappearing habitat, climate change, predators, life cycles, how things are made, characteristics and needs of living things, properties, motion, and weather. Within each of these areas of study lie potential stories.

Stories in science require the same kind of framing as in social studies. Look for the key events that children might live through in order to gain a greater insight into the tensions and processes involved in the science story. For example, impact on humans and human impact on scientific properties and events are possibilities for dramatic play.

The fact that dramatic play can anthropomorphize almost anything means that non-human things can talk with each other. Igneous and sedimentary rocks can dramatize their formation and discuss their similarities and differences. The stomach can talk to the intestines, and both can complain about the human in which they are located. Trees can talk about erosion, and even soils can argue about their merit. However, because stories in science tend to be non-human, they are more elusive. They rely on participants having a basic understanding of the qualities and nature of the material being personalized before dramatic play begins.

Stories in Science: Examples

- *Climate Change:* Drought has a severe impact on a community and so citizens discuss the need to find new sources of water.
- *Clean Water:* Students research how communities struggle to get clean water. Perhaps they negotiate with a local town official (teacher in role) to access a water source.
- *Characteristics and Needs of Living Things:* Beavers gather to discuss their frustration with humans breaking through their dams.
- *Life Cycles:* The life of a seed is enacted, as in the Eric Carle books *The Tiny Seed* and *The Hungry Caterpillar*.
- *Disappearing Habitat:* A fox (teacher in role) appears carrying a sign identifying land as sold for development and asks the children in role as animals for help in communicating concerns about habitat loss to humans.

Exploring Living Things in Science: Becoming Butterflies

Monarchs, Part 1

The Grade 1 students were excited about the butterfly larva coming to their classroom in a few weeks. They had been studying metamorphosis and were very familiar with the process. When the dramatist arrived they informed her of the details of transformation from caterpillar to butterfly. When she invited them to become caterpillars and go through the cycle, they immediately began crawling on their tummies. The dramatist moved among them, complimenting them on their abilities, and then called them back to the carpet.

Reviewing the next phase with them, the dramatist suggested that they find a place in the classroom where the caterpillar might attach itself in order to begin transforming into a pupa. They rushed off to claim a space and were reminded to be safe and not try to hang upside down. There was much discussion about the shape of the Monarch caterpillar as it hung in a *J* shape, as well as much experimentation with how they could make their bodies into a *J*. Because they were all playing safely, the dramatist simply observed and commented on the various strategies.

"What happens next?" she inquired. "They make a chrysalis," the children replied in unison. *"How can you show that process?"* the dramatist asked. Again, many suggestions and experiments were attempted, each child figuring out a different movement that satisfied his or her understanding of this stage. The dramatist circulated around the room, ensuring that each caterpillar spinning a chrysalis was safe.

How to emerge from a chrysalis

Satisfied that the class was sufficiently focused, the dramatist asked the children to demonstrate how the butterfly might emerge from the chrysalis. Eager to show their flying techniques, most of the children immediately launched themselves as butterflies and flew around the room. Calling them back to the carpet the dramatist asked them to describe and then show her how a butterfly emerges from the chrysalis. This time, much more slowly, the children demonstrated emerging — they had seen videos.

When they were back in their places, the dramatist began a narrative to help them slow down further. *"The caterpillar began to change inside the chrysalis. It noticed its eyes changing. It noticed legs suddenly appearing. It discovered that its body was transforming from something long and fat to something very skinny. But the most wonderful thing of all was that it could feel wings growing from here back."*

The narrative served to slow down the action and give it a new authenticity as the children explored the stages of movement. They continued with the slow pulsing of their wings and then took flight. Earlier they had made large flowers, and these had been scattered around the room. The dramatist's narration led them from flower to flower, sipping nectar.

The butterflies advocate for the bees

Monarchs, Part 2 The next day, when the children came in from recess, they noticed that their flowers were covered in garbage, and a large bottle marked with a poison sign sat empty nearby. The distressed butterflies gathered in the meadow (the carpet) for a meeting, eager to discuss what they had found. At the meeting the dramatist read a letter from the bees requesting that the butterflies help them tell the humans that the overuse of pesticides was making them sick. Much sincere discussion about how the butterflies could help ensued. The children, still in role as butterflies but really themselves, finally agreed that they would make posters and did so. (Another class investigating the same problem wrote notes to the staff and flew to the staffroom to put them in their mail boxes!)

In this story the children were invited to be the butterflies and live out their cycle, but they were also invited to consider an environmental issue. The crisis in the drama story was introduced by the dramatist, but the solution was the students' own. Dramatic play made possible a fluid discussion, where the students were both butterflies and themselves as they discussed the letter from the bees. There is a seamlessness to this kind of play.

How Dramatic Play Unfolds: Addressing Drought

The Rainforest, Part 4
In Parts 4 and 5, the rainforest unit involving students in Grades 1 to 3 comes to an end.

The next time they met in the clearing, the children had much more information about the serious impact that drought had had on the entire rainforest. The children requested that the story begin as it did the last time they met. In fact, several children had already found their "den" in the library, where they were having their dramatic play experience. Agreeing that this approach was a very good idea, the dramatist began the narrative again and watched as the animals responded with much authenticity. She summoned them to the clearing with a drum and marvelled at their focus.

Council in the clearing

"Welcome back, animals of the rainforest. I wonder if you have given any thought to the drought problem that we talked about the last time we met."

With the reminder that they were in a council meeting and that only one creature could speak while holding the drumstick, the children, one by one, suggested possible solutions to the drought situation. "A bird with a poky beak flies up in the sky and pokes the cloud and the rain comes down . . ." The dramatist affirmed this as a good idea but also noted to herself that this was an individual action. She needed to wait for that one suggestion that would build the story and engage all of the children. "We could send the monkey to the lake with a bucket and water things . . ."

The suggestions continued until a boy said, "We could do a rain dance."

"What is a rain dance?" the dramatist asked.

"We jump around and do stuff and it rains."

Flagging this as the potential next step, the dramatist heard the rest of the suggestions, and the council meeting drew to an end.

A creative solution

The teacher must balance the children's playfulness within a dramatic story with scientific fact and environmental phenomena, in this case, drought. The children had read several storybooks about drought, including *The Water Hole* by Graeme Base, and done basic research online. Solutions to drought, however, are difficult even for the best scientific researchers! In the case of animals in the rainforest, a rain dance seemed the most accessible and plausible route to take. At this point, the unit was story, not a scientific investigation, and for the animals in the forest, the rain dance was an important way for them to develop a satisfactory solution. It was also an opportunity to create a meaningful end to their story through movement.

Dancing their way into rain

The Rainforest, Part 5

Several days later a message appeared in the classroom. It read:

Dear Rainforest Animals,
I shared all your ideas with the wise python. She thought for a long, long time. She remembers a story told when she was a baby about a rain dance bringing rain. Can we do a rain dance?
— Serendipity Sloth [written for her by a monkey]

- A recommended resource is *Primary ETFO Arts: Introducing Dance, Drama, Music, and Visual Arts in the Primary Grades*. The 2013 book is published by the Elementary Teachers' Federation of Ontario.
- Consider also this helpful framework from Manitoba Education: *Kindergarten to Grade 8 Dance: Curriculum Framework of Outcomes*, available online at http://www.edu.gov.mb.ca/k12/cur/arts/docs/dance_k8.pdf.

The following week the children met in the gym for about an hour to organize a rain dance. Staying neutral and letting the children's suggestions shape each step of the way, the dramatist acted simply as the supporter of their ideas. The children chose to move in a circle, dipping up and down "to show the rain falling," and to gather in a group, lifting their hands and opening their mouths as they so often did to catch raindrops. After several practices the children settled on their choreography. The following day they shared their dance with another class.

It had been a dry spring and the teachers were hoping that it would rain the next day. It rained the following week, but by then, the children had moved on!

SUMMARY
- Choose a curriculum-based story that will capture the children's imaginations.
- Construct a framework using the five essential questions (see page 65).
- Approach the story through step-by-step play in concert with the children making suggestions.
- At the initial gathering, ensure that you present a problem capable of challenging the group to respond to it and solve it.
- Act as one of the group who keeps the dialogue going.
- Present the *who*, *what*, *where*, and *why* of the issue in your initial statement.
- Invite the class to organize the play space appropriately.
- Take the time to practice at various stages.
- Use the meeting to bring everyone together and to take the first steps in the story.

7 Teacher in Role

"Teaching in role is a strategy which a great many teachers have found extremely useful. It is most often used in whole group work . . . particularly if the role you take on functions as an obstacle which the class (or representatives of the class) have to find their way around by argument, persuasion and compromise."
— Brian Woolland, *The Teaching of Drama in the Primary School* (p. 55)

Teacher in role is by far the scariest, the most fun, and the most exciting way to work with children in dramatic play. The teacher transforming into someone else is readily accepted by children in Kindergarten and Grades 1 and 2. Familiar with play, they understand that play involves being in role and imagining themselves in a story. They usually join in with gusto, particularly if the teacher in role requires them to help or strangely enough, to be aggressive and mean spirited! They are quite willing to suspend their disbelief, even if you simply put on an apron or a hat, or change your voice. Students in Grades 3 and 4 may at first be more skeptical. They may require more preparation, but in the end, they, too, cannot resist the fun of playing with their teacher, who has perhaps turned into a mad scientist or a penguin concerned about climate change.

Dorothy Heathcote, who developed teacher in role with a wonderful understanding of story and children's capacity to play, was perhaps the most eloquent and provocative with this approach. As Betty Jane Wagner records:

One of Heathcote's most effective teaching ploys is her skillful moving in and out of role. She goes into role to develop and heighten emotion; she comes out of it to achieve distance and the objectivity needed for reflection. Thus she helps participants stir up and express emotion and a moment later set it aside and look at it coolly, growing what she calls a "cool strip" in their minds. (1998, 128)

Teacher in role is a way for you to present a problem, tension, dilemma, or idea to the class by taking on the attitude of a character (human or otherwise) in a fictional story, in a historical event, in the community, or in the past, present, or future. The intent of the role is to deepen the students' understanding of the circumstances and connect them empathetically and emotionally to the situation. Teacher in role, as in all dramatic play experiences, makes the issues more complex and invites students to work out problems or issues in detail through interaction and reflection. It should not be seen as an acting job: its main purpose is to engage the students as a group with the problems and tensions. The teacher in role plays inside the story and offers guidance when necessary, or elicits discussion to move the story along.

There are two main variations on teacher in role: (1) formal role, and (2) interactive role, which is the most demanding but rewarding form of teacher involvement in dramatic play. These are discussed below.

What Is a Formal Role?

A formal role is a way for you to prepare to take a more interactive role as teacher if you are at all hesitant about working together with children in dramatic play. It is more preplanned and controlled than an interactive role and much more focused on the personal story of an individual. It offers one point of view. Little response is required from the children.

In a formal role, the teacher tells the story from inside a character's particular point of view in order for children to empathize with the character and fully comprehend the impact of events on the person. The personal story is essentially a monologue as the character reflects on feelings and wonders openly about his or her situation.

A formal role requires you to research or imagine the backstory of an individual confronting a problem or an issue, and then to stay inside the story's emotional content and speak from the first-person singular. As in other dramatic play experiences, you would work between the lines of the story, imagining the dilemmas and predicaments that the character might be facing. You can study what is said and is not said in the source text to explore the feelings, hopes, and worries of the individual; consider other sources of information; and wonder aloud about the situation.

A formal role is an excellent way for you to assess what the children have learned at the end of a unit. If you play someone who is confused or does not fully understand what is happening, the children have an opportunity to help you with all the wisdom they have gleaned in their study. Although you are interacting with the children, they are responding to the formal role you are playing as themselves.

Because dramatic play can give voice to almost anything — animate or inanimate — you can present almost anything in a formal role. A magnet, for example, can wonder why it is attracted to certain things and ask the children what they know about the phenomenon. A seed might wonder what is happening as it feels the stretch upward and downward at the same time. Wondering or asking for help in a formal role is a delightful way to discover how children understand and articulate what they know. It is also less stressful than taking a full interactive role.

Planning for a Formal Role

The formal role usually requires research. Although you may be tempted not to do any research but instead to imagine a situation from a preconceived notion of what the individual might face, relying on clichés and stereotypes can erode the effectiveness of the formal role. Novels, children's books, diaries, historical accounts, photos, and videos will support your imaginative exploration of the individual's life. In choosing what to say, remember that dramatic play relies on things being difficult; that is, either a given situation is difficult in itself or you want the children to understand the complexity of a situation. Teacher in role should invite children to ponder the more serious questions that can be illuminated by the teacher telling the story from a personal perspective.

Taking the formal role need not mean a lengthy presentation. Sometimes, the children will be completely drawn in after listening to the individual for five minutes. Little is necessary in way of a costume, although a costume or costume piece can be as much support for the teacher to get into character in the classroom as for the actor on stage. If you intend to stop and start playing the role in order for the children to develop questions, choose something symbolic or simple to take on and off. A hat, scarf, apron, or cloak might suffice.

Ways to approach the role

To begin a formal role, always ask the students if they are willing to pretend that you are someone else when you put on a hat, change your voice, or sit in a particular place. You may need to encourage students in Grades 3 and 4 to willingly suspend their disbelief. They are often skeptical and may want to challenge, or test, the role. Students in earlier grades will have no problem with you going into role.

As in all dramatic play experiences, you will want to discuss their response to the character ahead of time and make sure that they use the same protocols that they would for a guest visiting the classroom. For example, you could arrange to have a student welcome the character as a guest or introduce the "guest" to the class. Even if your formal role is that of an unsavory character stepping into the classroom, setting up a gracious introduction will serve as a sharp contrast to the character's interaction with the children and subsequent exit.

Sometimes, planning questions with the children to ask the character can benefit you in the development of your monologue. If you know these questions ahead of time, you will gain a sense of what the students might want to hear from the character and can address the questions in your monologue. For example, in one instance, the teacher was in role as a tooth complaining about all the candies her person was eating. The children wanted to ask whether the tooth was scared of the dentist, whether it was loose, and whether jujubes hurt it more than M&Ms. Their questions made it clear to the teacher that the children were interested in the tooth expanding on their own experiences.

Planning the formal role with the children eases them into the process of the teacher becoming someone else and allows you to find out how they perceive the character and the character's situation. If you are playing an elderly person, for example, ask the children to help you know how to sit in your chair. They can shape you as they would in the sculpting game, or they can verbally describe how you might sit: "Your hands should be in your lap." "Your head should poke out more." The children might begin with what could be considered a stereotypical depiction of an elder, but the focus can shift as the role goes beyond simply the physical.

A symbolic piece of clothing or hand prop often helps children enter into a willing suspension of disbelief; it also supports your sense of the character. Removing the shawl or hat, or putting aside a bowl or photograph is a good way to indicate that you have returned to being yourself. You can then engage in a reflective conversation with the children about the person they have just met.

Some teachers use the element of surprise in presenting a role: for example, they tell the students that they can expect a visitor after recess but do not say who. They then enter the room in full costume. This kind of occasion is a lot of fun and children quite readily play along, but they often take much longer to get past the giggles and trick questions about where their teacher is or if you are "for real." They are slow to willingly suspend their disbelief. In choosing what approach to take, you will have to decide whether surprise and fun are what you want primarily or whether listening and reflection would be more beneficial to your students.

The Teacher in Formal Role: Examples

- A pioneer woman tells her story. She is lonely, homesick, and worried about the harvest. She wears an apron and holds a bowl of potatoes.
  Intention: To have students empathize with and focus on hardships and struggles
- An animal tells how it feels to have a dwindling habitat. The character has furry mittens or ears and may carry a sign announcing some kind of industry or development.
  Intention: To explore the full implications of loss of habitat
- Lurvy, in E. B. White's *Charlotte's Web*, tells what he has seen as a hired hand. The character wears a straw hat and carries a pail.
  Intention: To provide an insider's view of the farm along with suspicions of the animals
- A young tree becomes frightened when she notices her leaves changing. She wonders what is happening to her. The teacher in role as tree holds a branch and wears a twig-festooned hat.
  Intention: To assess how much the children have learned about the changing of leaves in the fall
- A tooth asks the class to help it write a note to the person in whose mouth it is to stop eating so many sweets. As a student teacher once prepared, the teacher in role wears a white shirt with a big black spot on it and a sticky-looking substance stuck to a sleeve.
  Intention: To invite the children to discuss healthy eating and brushing

Illustration of teacher in role as a tooth

Groaning. Not again! She's sent me another candy, and I'm trying my best to keep it away from that rotten spot, but it sure hurts. OOOOH! OUCH!

This has got to stop! I can't keep on eating these sweet things, or I will have to get pulled out and taken away by the Tooth Fairy. That might not be a bad idea, but I'd rather stay here with the other molars. Fillings aren't fun, but I could live with that. The molar next to me had a filling a long time ago, and he says it wasn't all that bad . . . better than the pain, that's for sure. What am I going to do . . . ?

The teachers holds her jaw for a moment. And then in comes another candy!

What's almost worse is, I've heard her mom ask her if she's brushed her teeth. She says yes, but I can tell you she hasn't. I would love a good brush right about now. I like that toothpaste, too. It always makes me feel fresh and new.

Is there anything that would get the message across that cavities are no fun? Do you have any idea of what I can do? Could you write a note for me? I'm not sure what it should say . . .

Your Role as Teacher in a Formal Role

When choosing a formal role, bear in mind that it is easier for a woman to be believed in the role of a man than for a man to be believed in the role of a woman.

When engaging in teacher in role, you are responsible for developing a character that is believable and accurate. Doing so will involve research — personal accounts are invaluable. When working with another culture, however, pursuing an issue or a specific story is preferable to trying to portray the culture or use an accent. For example, you may want to try a Scottish brogue or speak in broken English, but your skill with accents is not what matters. Instead, focus on the circumstances that the individual you are portraying faces. Teacher in role is *not* an acting job.

Ensure that you provide children with a clear picture of their guest. That means developing the opening statement, the most important part of your formal monologue, so that it indicates *who*, *what*, *where*, *when*, and *why* right at the beginning. It may also mean that you are careful to prepare them for your transformation and to sense when they are ready for you to begin. Opening a letter, peeling a potato, looking at a picture . . . will help you set the stage for the person you are to portray. A prop may also help with your own focus.

Beyond Facts to Empathy

Assume that the class is studying the building of the Canadian Pacific Railway and the role of Chinese workers. You want students to go beyond the facts to enter into a more empathetic understanding of the hardships the workers faced. To prepare, you might read aloud *Blood and Iron: Building the Railroad* by Paul Yee to your students or use the title from the I Am Canada series as background preparation for your role. Doing this will take you into the issues faced by the workers rather than any depiction of the culture.

Model appropriate practice. When children participate in dramatic play, we ask them to practice their roles, and in the same way, although not in the classroom, you will want to practice so that what you say has credibility and elicits the emotional response you are looking for from the children. Your practice may be at home in front of a mirror or with a colleague or someone else who can give you feedback. Preparing the first paragraph in writing is very helpful as it allows you to weed out unimportant material. When you present in a formal role, holding a script is fine as long as the paper is for reference and not read verbatim. A letter, however, can be read directly.

Seeking student help to prepare for teacher in role

These suggestions apply mainly to formal roles.

- Show possible costumes of several different styles and hand props for the students to decide which would best suit the role. Options include various kinds of hats, scarves, jackets, or items the character might carry. You could store such pieces in a tickle trunk, as noted in Chapter 4.
- Have the students coach you as to how you should stand, sit, move, and talk. Get them to show you as a group.
- Ask the children to advise you on where and how to begin playing your part. For example: Should you be frightened and reluctant to enter, hiding in a corner? Why do they think this?
- Make sure that the students are clear about how they are expected to listen and ask questions.
- Practice how they should greet you and where and how they should be in the classroom.
- Practice your entrance and their greeting. Doing this helps you become more comfortable in your role and anticipate how the students will respond.

Engaging the children

As noted above, in a formal role, you clearly define who you are, where you are, what your attitude is, what the problem is, and who the children represent. For example, as a tree you might introduce yourself as follows:

Holding two branches I am the youngest tree [who you are] in the park [where you are], and I am very frightened [your attitude]. I don't know what is happening to me and all the other trees! My beautiful leaves are changing color, and they are falling off [the problem].

I think I must be sick, but then so are all the other trees in the park. It's shocking! I've tried to keep my leaves green and I've tried to stick them back on, but nothing seems to work. I don't know where to turn, so I've come to you for help [the students' role]. I understand that you have been studying trees and you know about these things. Please help me. I don't want to be sick. Do you know what's happening to me?

In this example, the tree will not understand the process of leaves turning color and will need the children to explain this as best they can. The tree, insisting on keeping her leaves and having them green throughout the year, thus encourages the students to explain winter and cold and how the tree protects herself from freezing. Responses from the children may range from factual details to more fanciful ideas, but the teacher in role accepts both. The children's responses will provide ample material for follow-up.

When the explanations and discussions have been exhausted, the teacher will put down the branches she has been holding and step out of role. She can then ask the students what they could do to help the young tree feel better about the changes she is experiencing. No doubt, a variety of suggestions worthy of further development will emerge, and the children can explore some of these through learning centres, or stations, within the classroom. They could, for example, collect leaves and try to match the colors in a painting of fall trees to show the tree how beautiful fall is or chart how many leaves are yellow, how many are brown, and so on to show the tree how the colors are all unique and different.

The children may want to find out more about the youngest tree in the park and ask for her to return so that they can interview her and make a storybook. Having done some additional research, the teacher in role will, of course, reappear in order to appreciate all of these insights. The possibilities are many, but the point here is that the children have experienced the personification of a tree, which provides an excitement and motivation to take tree investigations further.

A Formal Role, Three Ways: Bully, Bystander, Bullied

The Grade 4/5 teacher and the guidance counsellor were concerned that one of the children in the class was being bullied. After much discussion on how to approach this sensitive topic, it was decided that the dramatist would play three formal roles: the bully, a bystander, and an individual being bullied. The intention behind presenting these roles was for the children to listen in on each of the character's thoughts and attitudes for discussion and reflective writing. This multiple role portrayal demonstrates the fluidity of dramatic play, which enables children to look at all sides of a story or event.

The bully began the monologue as follows:

Ha, ha. That little "twitch kid" . . . what a laugh. He sits there in class and it's like "twitch, twitch, twitch." It's hilarious. Me and my friends, we got him good the other day — pushed him up against the fence and he just stood there with his hands over his ears. Stupid little freak. He's such a wimp — sits up front on the bus with the girls — can you believe it!

The bully continued on with further stories of bullying but also gave some background about his home life and his desire to "take off" if and when his dad showed up again. The children listened intently.

The bystander began the monologue as follows:

I don't know. I was just there when he started just saying bad stuff about "the twitch kid," and he wouldn't stop. The kid put his hands over his ears so he couldn't hear but he kept at him and pulled his hands away and got right up close — right in his face — and kept yelling stuff. I guess I should have told him to stop, but I just stood there. I didn't even think to go get an adult like they tell us.

The bystander continued speaking, confessing that he took a photo of the incident on his cellphone that he sent around to friends because he thought it would be cool. He did not expect that it might go viral, but it did.

The person being bullied began the monologue as follows:

I guess it started mostly when I went into Grade 5. That Dwayne guy just zoomed in on me — him and his buddies. He's a big guy and he's mean that's for sure. I don't want to say that I'm chicken — it's more like I don't know what to do. I see him coming down the hall and I just freeze. It all started with him knocking my cap off every time he saw me and he'd say something like "twitch face" or "stupid ninny twitcher."

The victim continued speaking, expressing his feelings and his reluctance to talk about the situation with his mother and the teachers. He said he wanted to quit school but realized he couldn't. He concluded that all he could do was "keep hiding out whenever I can."

The students' participation in this teacher-in-role activity was to listen in on the thoughts of each of character. Listening gave them the opportunity to go deeper into the story of each and consider the difficulties and challenges each faced.

The discussion that followed the three-part presentation was rich and heartfelt, and the classroom teacher later affirmed that things changed in the classroom for the better.

What Is an Interactive Role?

For an interactive role, the teacher takes on a character or plans a character with the students, in order to engage the children in problem solving. As Brian Woolland (1993, 55) writes: "Teaching in role requires the teacher to play a role in the drama with the children for a specific purpose. The role itself should provide some focus for the drama. This could be as simple as entering the drama as a messenger and passing on information . . ."

Work in an interactive role tends to be much more improvised than in a formal role. Nonetheless, the same amount of research may be necessary in order to sketch in the details. The teacher in an interactive role usually begins playing with the children in role as they are confronting the issue they have decided to face. As a co-player, the teacher encourages discussion, problem solving, generation of ideas, and next steps.

The teacher may also want to switch roles in order to develop students' understanding of other perspectives in the story. For example, you may play the role of a fellow animal in order to gather the children (in role as animals) to discuss a particular situation that the children have identified. Once the children as animals have decided on a strategy for addressing the problem — say, loss of habitat — you may want to make the situation more complex by playing a role from another side of the story.

For example, Grade 1 students were in role as animals facing intrusion into their habitat by a lumber company. They devised a plan to dig holes around their homes so that the lumberjacks would fall into them. After a period of furious mimed digging, the classroom teacher, teaching assistant, and dramatist switched roles: instead of being part of the animal group, they became lumberjacks. They sauntered around the room, visiting each child's place of hiding, and commented on the strange holes, wondering what had made them. The animals' plan had been thwarted, and the children returned to their meeting place to plan again.

Improvising in Interactive Role: Examples

- *A threatened group meets in secret to discuss escaping from a tyrant king.*
  The teacher plays the role of the one who has called the meeting. Later, she plays the role of the tyrant king.
- *A municipal government meets to discuss a proposal for a housing development that will encroach on a much-used natural walkway.*
  The teacher plays the role of a council member asking questions and encouraging discussion; depending on the direction the children take, she later plans a role that makes their initial decision more complex.
- *Skilled workers in ancient Egypt gather to discuss the pharaoh's next big project.*
  The teacher plays the role of the vizier, who has received word that the workers must present the pharaoh with plans for yet another monument in his honor. The teacher then switches roles and becomes one of the skilled workers, helping to plan but also complaining about the amount of work and the pay. Later, the teacher may return as the vizier reporting that the pharaoh wants the plans immediately or their pay will be cut.

Planning an Interactive Role

Ask yourself which type of teacher role best facilitates the idea that you would like to explore with the children. Who will you be?

For an interactive role, the teacher is most often one of the group or a secondary character in an event. Such a role is dependent on the dramatic story, of course, but examples include being a member of a family or of a group of animals, settlers, town councillors, or workers in a community. The character is someone who can shed more light on the problem, provide some insight, and encourage conversation, plans, and decision making. On the other hand, adopting the role of an authority figure, such as the king or the head of a company, can be a deliberate strategy to force the children to rethink their plans and talk about the experience.

The teacher in an interactive role can also play the character next in line to the authority figure. This role may involve relaying messages and providing more challenges to the group as the character moves back and forth between them and the imagined authority. For example, the royal representative might say: *"I asked the King, and he was very upset with your demand. He said that he does not entertain peasants who make demands."* This message complicates the situation and challenges the children to try another strategy.

In dramatic play involving Egyptian workers, the teacher as vizier can simply relay information from the workers to the pharaoh and back again, giving advice. As one of the workers, the teacher can play more directly within the scenario, encouraging questions, promoting discussion, and working towards possible solutions. If the teacher were to play the role of pharaoh with the children, it would be to demonstrate the ruler's power and increase the tension in the story.

Be careful when you choose to adopt a powerful role — for example, the queen, the head of the company, or the one in command. Unless you are in a formal role doing a monologue, playing the powerful role at the beginning of dramatic play can limit the direction the students take. This kind of role often comes later in the dramatic play when children decide to present their case to the higher authority.

When developing your role, consider the following questions:

- What are the main attitudes of the character?
- How could the role make the issue more complex and emotional?
- Is there enough opportunity for all the students to participate equally?

How Dramatic Play Unfolds: The Timid Triceratops

A Kindergarten class was very interested in dinosaurs. They had learned the names of most and could identify and tell the difference between the largest and the smallest. They had even measured the size of a tyrannosaurus rex in the hallway. The teacher, however, wanted to involve the children in a play experience and wondered if the dramatist playing a role might provide them with an interesting challenge.

Belief in the dinosaur

Because this approach was new to the students, the dramatist brought a number of items that she thought might help them believe in the transformation from human to dinosaur. She showed the children a green tuque, a paper ruff to go around her neck, and green mittens, along with a number of other dinosaur-like things to wear.

The dramatist asked, *"Which do you think would help you believe that I am a dinosaur?"* There was some discussion, but it was unanimous that the ruff and the mittens would be sufficient. The children then identified the dinosaur as a "triceratops," and the dramatist knew that the willing suspension of disbelief had occurred.

Having determined the costume, the dramatist went on to tell the children that she was a frightened triceratops. She asked where they thought she might want to be in the classroom. A number of them pointed to the back of the room and insisted that behind the bookcase was a good place to be. They giggled with

Students in a Grade 4/5 class were in role as Métis in the Red River Settlement in 1816. They wrote a petition to present to Governor Robert Semple, and a delegation was chosen to meet with the governor, who was to be the dramatist. After recess, however, one of the boys had taken up his post at the desk designated for the governor. He donned the top hat and sat with great authority at a desk strewn with papers. While the rest of the class was preparing, the dramatist asked whether the student was ready to hold firm and not give in to Métis demands. The student as governor gave a resounding "yes," so the dramatist chose to become his assistant and not intervene. The governor said very little to the delegation that approached him. Its members grew more and more frustrated as he pushed the papers around on his desk and pretended not to hear their demands!

All Aboard!

Assume that your role involves planning a trip to the planets. In this instance, make sure that all of the students are on the space ship and have something to look after. You will journey with them to help make observations, deal with organization, and address tensions.

Dinosaur Roar

excitement and anticipation as the dinosaur hid and began to cry. She could hear them coming closer and tentatively peeked around the corner, curious to see what they might do next. A little girl moved forward, extending her hand, and said: "Don't cry, Dinosaur. We won't hurt you."

Slowly, the dramatist moved out from behind the shelves. As she did so, the children gathered around her, took her hand, and led her to the carpet.

Before she told them her story, the dramatist wanted the children to build trust with her as the dinosaur, and she was curious to hear how they would do this. Some empathized immediately and wanted to know why she was crying. Several argued that they should leave her alone for a while until she felt like talking. One girl held the dinosaur's "hand" and stroked it silently.

Taking on a fierce foe

Finally, the triceratops told the children her story: A tyrannosaurus rex had moved into her swamp and was so big, so loud, and so threatening that she was very frightened and ran away. Now she was lonely and wanted to go back home.

"What should I do?" she cried.

There were many suggestions. "You could stay with us." "You can eat grass — there's lots of grass." Others suggested that the triceratops come home with them, stay in the library, or go to the zoo. When she declared again that she just wanted to go back to her own swamp and couldn't they help in some way, a child blurted out, "We can make scary masks and turn ourselves into monsters and scare the tyrannosaurus rex away."

Seeing this as a great opportunity with multiple learning potentials, the dramatist asked the children if they were really willing to face the fierce tyrannosaurus rex. Their response was to rise as one, find paper and markers, and make fierce masks. Out of role, the dramatist and the classroom teacher circulated to assist with holes for eyes and ties to keep their masks on while the children talked about the dinosaur's plight.

A really big scare

Several days later the Kindergarten children met with the dinosaur again, this time to practice the loud and scary roar that one of the children had suggested. The teacher had, in the meantime, arranged mats, benches, and hula hoops in the gym to simulate a journey through a swamp. She had also asked the principal to be in the gym office and on cue roar like a tyrannosaurus rex and make the sound of the meat-eating dinosaur running away.

There was lots of tension in the excursion to the gym and through the swamp. The children suggested what the mats, benches, and hula hoops might be and how they might proceed through them, getting stuck, walking along a log (and falling off), leaping over water until they and the dinosaur finally arrived behind a hill (benches stacked one on the other).

They waited and, sure enough, they heard the smacking lips and munching of the tyrannosaurus rex. On the count of three the children gave their best roar. It echoed around the gym.

Did it work? There was a brief pause. Then, over the loudspeaker came the booming voice of the principal echoing through the gym as he declared that he was "getting out of the swamp for good."

The children, startled by the surprising and very loud voice coming from nowhere, fled back to the classroom in terror! The embarrassed principal was quick to come to the door and apologize for using the microphone and not his normal voice, and the dramatist was quick to gather the panicked children to discuss being afraid, reminding them of the promise to help and asking them if they would like to try again.

Having recovered from the initial shock, the children all agreed that they felt brave enough to try again.

This time the children traversed the swamp with much tension, and this time the principal responded in his normal loud voice from the gym office. Hearing the tyrannosaurus rex fleeing, the children cheered and went back to the classroom to talk further about risk, helping, fear, and courage, and what fun it was to play together.

SUMMARY

- Decide which kind of teacher role will tell the story best: formal or interactive.
- Research and imagine the backstory. This research might be your own for a formal role or be research done by the children as their dramatic story evolves.
- Plan symbolic pieces of clothing and/or props. For a formal role, you would choose these, but in an interactive role, you would likely discuss what the symbolic pieces should be with the students.
- Prepare the opening statement of the story: establish *who*, *what*, *where*, *when*, and *why* for a formal role. In an interactive role, these elements would be clarified as the story evolves.
- If you are adopting an interactive role, be prepared to question, challenge, discuss, and participate with the children.
- Prepare to play more than one role if doing so will bring further depth to the dramatic play.

References

Board of Studies New South Wales. 2006. *New South Wales Creative Arts Syllabus, Early Stage 1*. Retrieved from Board of Studies NSW. http://k6.boardofstudies.nsw.edu.au.

Booth, David. 2005. *Story Drama: Creating Stories through Role Playing, Improvising, and Reading Aloud*. Markham, ON: Pembroke.

Cornett, Claudia E. 2010. *Creating Meaning through Literature and the Arts: Arts Integration for Classroom Teachers*, 4th ed. Newmarket, ON: Pearson.

Dewey, John. 1938. *Experience and Education*. Toronto: Collier-MacMillan Canada.

Edwards, Carolyn, Lella Gandini, and George Forman, eds. 1998. *The Hundred Languages of Children: The Reggio Emilia Approach to Early Childhood Education*, 2nd ed. Norwood, NJ: Ablex.

Fox, Jill Englebright, and Robert Schirrmacher. 2015. *Art and Creative Development for Young Children*, 8th ed. Stanford, CT: Cengage Learning.

Hewes, Jane. 2006. *Let the Children Play: Nature's Answer to Early Learning*. Montreal: Early Childhood Learning Knowledge Centre. Retrieved from www.ccl-cca.ca/pdfs/ECLKC/lessons/LearningthroughPlay_LinL.pdf.

Johnson, Liz, and Cecily O'Neill, eds. 1984. *Dorothy Heathcote: Collected Writings on Education and Drama*. London: G. B. Hutchinson Education.

Jones, Elizabeth, and John Nimmo. 1995. *Emergent Curriculum*. Washington, DC: National Association for the Education of Young Children.

Kelly, Robert, and Carl Leggo. 2008. *Creative Expression, Creative Education: Creativity as a Primary Rationale for Education*. Calgary, AB: Detselig.

Levin, Diane E. 2003. "Beyond Banning War and Superhero Play: Meeting Children's Needs in Violent Times." *Young Children*. Retrieved from National Association for the Education of Young Children: www.naeyc.org.

Manitoba Child Care Program. 2009. *Early Returns: Manitoba's Early Learning and Child Care Curriculum Framework for Preschool Centres and Nursery Schools*. Retrieved from http://www.gov.mb.ca/fs/childcare/pubs/early_returns_en.pdf.

Manitoba Education. 2011. *Kindergarten to Grade 8 Drama: Manitoba Curriculum Framework of Outcomes*. Retrieved from www.edu.gov.mb.ca/k12/cur/arts/drama.

McCain, Margaret Norrie, J. Fraser Mustard, and Stuart Shanker. 2007. *Early Years Study 2: Putting Science into Action*. Toronto: Council for Early Child Development.

Miller, Carole S., and Juliana Saxton. 2004. *Into the Story: Language in Action through Drama*. Portsmouth, NH: Heinemann.

Ontario Ministry of Education. 2009. *The Ontario Arts Curriculum, Grades 1 to 8: The Arts.* Retrieved from http://www.edu.gov.on.ca/eng/curriculum/elementary/arts18b09curr.pdf.

Paley, Vivian G. 2004. *A Child's Work: The Importance of Fantasy Play.* Chicago: University of Chicago Press.

———. 2011. "A Conversation with Vivian Gussin Paley." Retrieved from National Association for the Education of Young Children: www.naeyc.org.

Shaughnessy, Michael E. 1998. "An Interview with E. Paul Torrance: About Creativity." *Educational Psychology Review* 10 (4): 441–52.

Vygotsky, Lev S. 1978. *Mind in Society: The Development of Higher Psychological Processes.* Cambridge, MA: Harvard University.

Wagner, Betty Jane. 1998. *Educational Drama and Language Arts: What Research Shows.* Portsmouth, NH: Heinemann.

Wallas, Graham. 1926. *The Art of Thought.* New York: Harcourt Brace.

Warner, Christine. 1997. "The Edging In of Engagement: Exploring the Nature of Engagement in Drama." *Research in Drama Education: The Journal of Applied Theatre and Performance* 2 (1): 21–24.

Woolland, Brian. 1993. *The Teaching of Drama in the Primary School.* New York: Longman.

Index

art, augmenting understanding through, 46
assessment
    children's commitment, 20–21
    practice, 29

belief/believability
    augmenting understanding through art, 46
    blank paper, 47
    building, 41–52
    dramatic play, 50–52
    first-person singular, 48
    narration, 44
    play energy and theatre practice, 41–42
    researching details, 45–46
    rumors and imagining, 44–45
    space, 42–44
    teacher's role, 49–50
    writing in role, 48–49
blank paper
    building belief through use of, 47
    developing story through drawing, 15
    potency of, 72
bodily knowing, 13
bullying, 84–85

characters
    getting into character, 67
    story possibilities, 8
    identifying, 15–16
children's commitment, 20–21
co-construction, 9
    step-by-step experience, 69–70
comprehension
    building on, 57–58
    pausing, 23–24
context, 67
creative energy, 17
creative process (creativity)
    becoming animals example, 13–14

dramatic play, 11, 15–17
    four stages, 10–11
    imaginative thinking, 11–12
    launching activity, 17
    pausing to reflect and experiment, 12
    teacher's role, 14–15
curriculum
    approaches, 66–68
    character and context, 67
    dramatic play, 64, 66, 77–78
    example, 71–73
    framework for investigation, 64–65
    historical stories, 70–71, 73–74
    issues to explore, 66
    meeting in role, 67–68
    play space, 66
    science, 74–75
    social studies, 68–70

deeper responses, 21–22
discussing and pauses, 25–26
dramatic play experiences
    Animals under the Mitten, 50–51
    Cinderella the Servant, 56–57
    The Crew of La Grand Hermine, 45–46, 73–74
    Dinosaur Roar, 87–89
    The Fairy Tale, 5–6, 43
    Firefighting, 69–70
    Greek Gods, 37–38
    Imprisoned in the Tower, 63
    Leaving Home for a New Life, 71–73
    The Lost Goose, 20, 21–22
    Monarchs, 75–76
    The Rainforest, 27–28, 38–40, 51, 77–78
    Regaining the Castle, 15–17, 49
    The Treasure Map, 62
dramatist, 9
drawing
    developing the story, 15

portraits, 46
sustained observation, 33–34
dressing up, 46

embodiment of experience, 13
empathy, 83
experience, 6
embodiment of, 13
experimentation, 12
example, 16–17

"filling in the picture," 45
first-person singular, 48
focus and control
physical games and activities for, 31–33
working towards, 30–31
formal role
approaching, 81–82
described, 80
engaging children, 83–84
examples, 82, 84–85
planning for, 80–82
students' help in, 83
teacher's role, 83–84
framework
establishing for investigation, 64–66
example, 71–73
historical stories, 70–71
questions, 65
Freeze Frame, 22

guided looking, 33–34

historical stories
coloring in picture, 71
experiencing, 73–74
framing, 70–71

idea gathering, and pausing, 26
illumination
becoming animals example, 13
described, 11
teacher in role, 81
imagination (imaginative thinking), 11–12
rumors and, 44–45
willing suspension of disbelief, 19–20
improvisation/improvising, 60–61
beginning, 61
interactive role, 86
object base, 62

planting a letter, 61
prompting, 61–62
research, 61
setting, 61–62
incubation
becoming animals example, 14
described, 11
insight, and pausing, 23–24
inspiration, 10, 11
integrating contributions, 21–22
interactive role
described, 85–86
improvising examples, 86
planning, 86–87

listening
direct approach, 25
methods, 24–25
next steps, 24–25
pausing for discussion, 25
role playing, 25
lived-through experiences, 53, 54
look-draws, 34

masks, 46
meaning, and pausing, 23–24
Mirrors, 23

narration, 44
natural response, 7
neutral and curious, 37
"not for real" aspect, 18

objects
improvisation, 62
play space, 66
outcomes, 8

partnership, 7–8
pausing
benefits, 25–26
comprehension, meaning, and insight, 23–24
dealing with problems, 23–24
deepening understanding, 26
discussion and planning, 25–26
example, 24
experimentation, 12
gathering ideas, 26
listening, 25
reflecting, 12, 23–24
signal, 23

perspectives, 54
    different, 58–59
planning, pausing for, 25–26
planting a letter, 61
play energy, 41–42
portraits, 46
practice
    dramatic play, 37–40
    drawing, 33–34
    focus and control, 30–31
    importance of, 29–40
    side-coaching, 34–35
    slow motion, 36
    slowing down, 29
    space and, 43–44
    sustained observation, 33–34
    taking small steps, 30
    teacher's role, 36–37, 83
    theatre, 41–42
preparation
    becoming animals example, 13, 14
    described, 11
process, 18
props
    mimed versus symbolic, 70
    producing, 46

reflection, 12, 23–24
Reggio Emilia approach, 9
research
    details and, 45–46
    improvising with, 61
    preparing for formal role, 83
risk taking, 12
role playing (roles)
    changing roles, 58
    fluidity, 17
    formal, 80–85
    interactive, 85–87
    listening, 25
    meeting establishment, 67–68
    teachers, 79–89
    writing, 48–49
rumors, 44–45

science
    exploring living things, 75–76
    finding story in, 74–75
Sculptor and Clay, 22–23
setting, 61–62

side-coaching, 20, 34–35
sketching, 46
slow motion, 36
slowing down, 29
social studies
    example, 69–70
    finding story in, 68–70
space
    defining, 66
    practicing in, 43–44
    using to suspend disbelief, 42–44
Statues, 31–32
story/stories
    children's interest in, 53
    choosing, 55–56
    classic, 59–60
    dramatic play, 62–63
    expanding understanding, 57–59
    going deeper, 56–57
    improvising, 60–62
    perspectives, 54
    possibilities, 8, 53
    staying inside, 55
    teacher's role, 59
    working with text, 53–54
storytelling
    dramatic play and, 7
    drawing and, 15
subtleties of stillness, 33
sustained observation, 33–34
    value of, 33–34
sword fighting, 36

tableaux, 32–33
Tapping In, 45, 55, 58
teachers
    beginning of play and, 26–27
    building belief and, 49–50
    creative process and, 14–15
    dramatic play and, 18
    partnership with learners, 7–8
    practice and, 36–37
    in role, 79–89
    within story, 59
teachers in role
    dramatic play, 87–89
    formal role, 80–85
    intent, 79–80
    interactive role, 85–87
    variations, 80
theatre

balancing play energy and practice, 41–42
    dramatic play and, 7, 8
thinking
    co-construction, 9
    imaginative, 11–12
"tickle trunk," 46
transcription, 48

understanding
    augmenting through art, 46
    expanding, 57–59
    pausing for, 26
unknown outcomes, 8

value of play, 6–7
verification
    becoming animals example, 14
    described, 11

warming up, 22–23
whole group, 18–19
willing suspension of disbelief, 19–20, 29, 30, 41
    using space, 42–44
writing in role, 48–49